Listen to
Their Voices

Also by Mickey Pearlman

CO-AUTHOR

Inter/View: Talks with America's Writing Women
(*A Voice of One's Own* in paperback),
with Katherine Usher Henderson

Tillie Olsen, with Abby H. P. Werlock

EDITOR

American Women Writing Fiction:
Memory, Identity, Family, Space

Mother Puzzles: Daughters and Mothers
in Contemporary American Literature

The Anna Book: Searching for Anna in Literary History

Listen to Their Voices

Twenty Interviews with Women Who Write

Mickey Pearlman

W · W · NORTON & COMPANY

NEW YORK   LONDON

Copyright © 1993 by Mickey Pearlman
All rights reserved
Printed in the United States of America
First Edition

The text of this book is in 10/13 Berkeley Old Style Book
with the display set in Berkeley Old Style Bold.
Composition and manufacturing by Maple-Vail Book Manufacturing Group.
Book design by Margaret M. Wagner.

Library of Congress Cataloging-in-Publication Data
Pearlman, Mickey
Listen to their voices : twenty interviews with women who write /
Mickey Pearlman.
p. cm.
1. Women authors, American—20th century—Interview.
2. Women and literature—United States—History—20th century.
3. American literature—Women authors—History and criticism.
I Title.
PS151.P415 1992,
810.9'9287'0904—dc20   92–14025

ISBN 0-393-03442-9

W. W. Norton & Company, Inc., 500 Fifth Avenue, New York, N.Y. 10110
W. W. Norton & Company Ltd., 10 Coptic Street, London WC1A 1PU

1 2 3 4 5 6 7 8 9 0

For Deena Stutman and Judy Sterling Weissel

"I can no other answer make but thanks,
And thanks; and ever thanks."

Twelfth Night
William Shakespeare

Contents

Contents

Introduction

INTERVIEWING women who write can be exhausting, intellectually demanding, and even logistically complicated. Nearly always, it is also fun—in spite of too many Greyhound bus trips, missed plane connections, and tape recorders that refuse to function. But when it works as planned, a good interview elicits insights about the writer and her work that are valuable both to other writers and to serious readers.

The choice of whom to interview, from a constantly replenished abundance of exciting choices, was complicated; it was based entirely on personal taste, an unscientific response to my own reading. I interviewed those women whose writing seems to me contemporary and topical, but also enduring; racially and ethnically specific, but also universal; often painful but at the same time cathartic.

I also wanted to present a cross section of the women being published in America today, without making any specific writer into a spokesperson for a particular ethnic, racial or religious group. In that spirit, there are interviews with Chinese-American, Japanese-American, Filipino-American, African-American, and Native American writers—women whose ethnic or racial background is usually linked (not always to their satisfaction) by a hyphen to the word "American." These so-called hyphenated writers speak openly about their dilemma: their feelings of alliance with writers of similar background and the frustration of being compared with them. When Cynthia Kadohata hears about the success of her "fellow" Asian-American, for instance, her first instinct is to say, "Go Gish." But she also has strong feelings about being pigeonholed. "Sometimes I want that identification, but not always, ... and I don't like people saying you have to be an 'Asian writer,' " as she believes reviewers do. Jessica Hagedorn simply says, "If my characters happen to be Filipino and they have to go back and forth [to the Philippines] because that's where the story takes them, it's fine with me. And if people say, 'Oh, she's the Filipino writer ... it's not my problem." Joy Harjo, who has a growing audience among all groups of Americans, says that her "first audience, ... or the inner circle, is, of course, my people. But I am an American citizen and I am a citizen of the world and of the universe. And I think my work addresses common concerns in its own very particular ways."

As usual, Grace Paley, who has watched the growing number of hyphenated writers, sums it up: "They're the new people, shining a light on what to them is hidden from the rest of the world, ... so they are telling it to us. What a writer is, really, is someone who tells the truth in the language of the country they're in, and sustains that language, and invigorates that language, ... and keeps lighting up what isn't known."

It will also be clear immediately to the readers of this collection that none of the twenty writers chosen for it is producing what Anne Rice calls "the tired ... small novel of manners about upper-middle-class-man-has-midlife-crisis-in-Ann-Arbor." The writers here chronicle what women see as everyday reality, and that reality often involves loss. For instance, Jayne Anne Phillips talks about the deaths of her mother and grandmother from lung cancer (perhaps related to radon poisoning), and Susan Kenney discusses her husband's struggle with cancer, familiar to the readers of her novel *Sailing*. Cancer, she says, "wouldn't be my choice of subject if I hadn't been handed it; I didn't choose the subject; it chose me." That is equally true for Terry Tempest Williams in *Refuge,* a memoir that draws a parallel between the rise of the water in the Great Salt Lake and the rising incidence of breast cancer in the state of Utah, with special emphasis on the women in her family. Shirley Abbott's memoir, *The Bookmaker's Daughter,* describes her childhood in Arkansas and her complicated relationship with her now-dead father who "made book" in Hot Springs, and Margot Livesey struggles with the job of finding out who her parents, both of whom died early in her life, really were. As she says, "It's disturbing to realize how little you can know of one of your parents," and "it's a real lesson in how quickly people disappear."

Like those in a previous collection called *A Voice of One's Own* (in its paperback version), the twenty interviews in *Listen to Their Voices* are not in question and answer form. The interview in essay form, it seems to me, allows more flexibility, depending, as it does, on the interviewer's ability to gain the writer's trust—in a matter of minutes—and on many other intangible factors: the match in mood, style, sense of humor, and shared interests; and the impact of the sometimes unsettling setting *on* that mood. The narrative form allows the reader to experience some of these missed or made connections. Most writers, it should be noted, are private people, often isolated by choice, and they spend a lot of time staring at computer screens or blank sheets of paper. This collection allowed some of them to make public (often unexpected) statements about politics, sexual harassment, race, or publishing.

All of the writers, however, seemed to be concerned with certain ideas. They spoke about the influence of audience, the creative process, and their role as witnesses. Much to my surprise, discussions about religion—Paley on Judaism, Williams on her Mormon background, Hagedorn on Catholicism as observed in the Philippines, Olds on Episcopalians and penance, and Janette Turner Hospital on her Pentecostal childhood in Queensland—

permeate the collection. These topics, I believe, were energized both by discussions of childhood and the search for order in the often chaotic late twentieth century.

Almost without exception, these writers pay attention to the increasing violence perpetrated against and experienced by women across the globe; in the bibliographies following each interview there are an extraordinary number of novels, short stories, memoirs, and poetry collections in which rape, incest, and other forms of abuse, appear. Smiley's *A Thousand Acres,* Olds's *The Father,* Hagedorn's *Dogeaters* are only few examples.

Much, too, is revealed about the persistence of childhood traumas. Janette Turner Hospital felt "like a space traveler" who daily moved from her secluded, Pentecostal home to the "very macho, philistine, hedonistic male culture" of Australian public school." Melinda Worth Popham spent hours in the basement of her Kansas City home, working at a "silent" Remington typewriter, herself silent because of a disabling stutter. Lucille Clifton, whose parents suffered from epilepsy, understood intellectual dislocation and emotional disruption at an early age.

THERE is considerable discussion, too, about a writer's decision to choose one genre (short stories instead of novels or poetry instead of prose) by Jayne Anne Phillips, Sharon Olds, and Susan Kenney. Lois Lowry and Lucille Clifton talk about writing for children, and Terry Tempest Williams and Shirley Abbott discuss the writing of memoir. Abbott says it depends on "trying to examine my past in such a way that it will have value for other people and will help other people examine their own past."

The issue of whether and how and if women should write, discussed at length in *A Voice of One's Own,* seems to be largely absent here. Interestingly, few of the writers talked about the struggle of raising children, or sustaining a marriage, as an almost impossible balancing act when those jobs are combined with writing. This seemed to be a nonissue, and I can only surmise that for this group of writers (only four of whom do *not* have children), that conflict seems to be resolved.

Instead, the writers in *Listen to Their Voices* concentrate on mining their deep and sometimes invasive memories. These memories, a writer's raw material (combined as always with invention and transformation), are the genesis of fiction and poetry. Of course writing also evolves from lived or observed experience, which Melinda Worth Popham pictures as "going in the big part of a funnel. . . . What finally comes through are these little grains of experience, . . . the memories that you really work with." In this collection at least, many of those "grains of experience" are the deaths of one or both parents, and the interviews make clear how both childhood and adult wounds are used as impulse to creation and as creation itself.

It is in interviews with Jane Smiley and Anne Rice that issues related to the process of writing and the complications of publishing emerge most fully. Sue Miller, whose novels *The Good Mother* and *Family Pictures* were sold to film or television producers for large amounts of money, speaks pragmatically about priorities. She advises all writers dreaming of lucrative film deals to follow Ernest Hemingway's advice: throw your book over the California border, pick up the money, and go back home and write. Anne Rice agrees. "You either release the rights or not, and once you do that, let it go." Rice speaks for many of the writers in this collection who want more involvement with production and marketing decisions that affect their work. And because her novels enjoy such popular success, she goes the farthest when she says, "At this point in my life I try to avoid any sort of editing [at the publishing house] because I edit my own work almost obsessively as I write. And what really interests me is *not* collaborative art; it's the vision of one writer." Jane Smiley is equally outspoken about favoritism to male writers in the publishing world: "As far as promoting [and the acquisition of books] is concerned, there is a kind of cronyism. In deals between editors and writers, the editors bring money to the table and the writers bring adventures—very masculine adventures— -. . .and they trade something that's really quite abstruse for something that's really quite tangible."

These comments suggest one of the most surprising strains in many of the interviews in *Listen to Their Voices*. If it is not exactly anger, what is being expressed here is a certain ambivalence and dissatisfaction with aspects of publishing, issues that writers frequently discuss at length with each other.

Finally, it's clear that writers are emotionally and intellectually connected; you don't have to spend much time with this group to see their commitment to each other's work (and to what I have personally been trying to accomplish in many years of interviewing women who write). That connection is immensely gratifying. Time and again, the first question asked of me was, "How is————doing? Is she writing? When is her next book coming out?" Since I served as the link among the writers, it became almost a commonplace for me to be given messages to deliver and words of support to impart. I was greatly encouraged by this sense of community in a time when bonds and connections seem to be breaking down at a furious pace.

As I was preparing this collection, I happened upon a poem by Linda Hogan, a Chickasaw activist and writer, called "Our Houses." It helped me to focus on the reasons why I wanted to spend the last several years listening to the voices of women who write. It now speaks clearly to what I heard and what the reader will hear in these pages:

> When we enter the unknown
> of our houses,
> go inside the given up dark
> and sheltering walls alone
> and turn out the lamps
> we fall bone to bone in bed.

Neighbors, the old woman who knows you
turns over in me
and I wake up
another country. There's no more
north and south.
Asleep, we pass through one another
like blowing snow,
all of us,
all.

Mickey Pearlman
September, 1992

Acknowledgments

NO ONE works on a book for a year and a half (and all the books that preceded it) without the emotional support of many people. I want to acknowledge especially the longtime friendship and cheerleading talent of Sanda Cohen, Sandra Appleman, and Arlene Hirschfelder, and the many welcome hoorahs offered at precipitous moments by Abby and Jim Werlock, Jill Shanker, Helen Pike Bauer, Myra Kelinson, Michael Flamini, Carole Weaver, Linda Occhino, Jerry Bauer, and Roberta White. Special thanks go to my editor, Carol Houck Smith, who richly deserves her illustrious reputation in the publishing community.

Listen to
Their Voices

Grace Paley

IF YOU are going to a tiny wooded village in Vermont called Thetford Hill to interview Grace Paley, you might consider stashing away a small supply of Valium in your suitcase. You'll need it if you choose to ride in a car with the unique and beloved New York writer who "lived in the Bronx for twenty years and then on 11th Street [in Greenwich Village] for forty years." Suffice it to say that Paley, who loves children—hers and everybody else's—frequently looks out the side window at them while she is driving, not always in her lane. When you discover that a large truck is coming directly at you—since you are driving in his lane—you might try to energize whatever navigational capabilities you still possess for the rest of the trip. (Try to forget about the part where she stops the car in the middle of the highway to talk to her stepdaughter's husband, who is from Somalia. Since he is carrying his newborn baby, he quite intelligently declines a lift.)

There's also the problem of Paley's schedule. While you are sitting in the Hanover Inn near Dartmouth College, ready to order lunch (with your tape recorder neatly set up and ready to go), she will suddenly remember that she is the guest of honor at another lunch, taking place at this exact moment, in another village, fifteen rollicking miles away. Thanks to the hostess's good nature, you both end up eating there. That's *after* you've driven up and down several roads, through the woods, looking for the house: "I'll recognize it; don't worry!" Of course there's always the possibility that you're already running late on your schedule because Paley has promised to write a piece for "the Quakers," and since it's now several weeks overdue, you've been looking for a fax machine in White River Junction, Vermont, the nearest technological metropolis. When Paley borrows your telephone calling card (since she forgot hers), to call "the Quakers" in Pennsylvania for their fax number, she somehow calls Utah instead. Since she's already two hours late for your interview, this will hardly matter.

All of this, of course, is what might be called classic Grace Paley. The consummate peace activist, with her curly white hair flying, has probably lost track of how many times she was arrested in the sixties during protests against American involvement in Vietnam, at marches against the use of nuclear power, and at rallies for women's rights. At sixty-nine she may be slowing down a bit, (doing "less now, because I'm really a little more tired"), although this is not noticeable to any normally active mortal. In any case, and under any circumstances, you will treasure any time that you spend with this irresistible woman.

Paley lives in a sprawling country house, with a large and comforting living room, that is surrounded by farmland that her husband Bob "gave to a young guy with very little land, who is going to use it for a few years." There are sheep, whose "major job is to make doo-doo on the grass." She says that she's "very moved by living in the country because I've been given the gift of having some kind of rural sense. I loved being the city writer, 'the New York City writer,' and I feel it, but now I have the gift of this place, of a certain amount of country life among real country people, not suburban people." Needless to say, the seemingly bucolic stillness of the Vermont landscape has not quieted Paley's activism in any noticeable way. True to her history, she's "been involved since 1977 in ecological things, one of my concerns, and I've been arrested with Bob many times at Seabrook [the nuclear facility in New Hampshire]. It's my nature to get to what is being done and to try to do it, and so I've been involved in what's going on here. I'm on the recycling committee. . . . It's the closest thing for me to being in New York. You get out, right down there near the school where they do the recycling, and the people all come, sort of like being on the street corner or something. Otherwise, you could live here for a year and not see a soul or just bump into them in the post office one at a time. So the recycling is good because they all come with their garbage and . . . tell you what's going on. . . . It's a beautiful place, like a laundromat or something."

Paley also does "a lot of work around here. I have a big garden: We grow a lot of food, and I freeze a lot. . . . I hardly ever invite anyone for dinner, . . . but anyone who is around, I'll feed. . . . I do stuff." (Earlier I've had a tour of the local health food co-op, where Paley is also a member.) At this point in the interview the phone rings and Paley returns to report that "my friend Carol [Emswiller] just called me from Montpelier to tell me that tomorrow night at seven the Women's Center is having a public forum on the Clarence Thomas confirmation hearings and that she just renamed the Ethan Allan room, where they are going to meet, the Anita Hill room. So I'll probably go to that forum. . . .

Did you read my story called 'Is Country Life Boring?' . . . There's plenty to do up here," she reports. No doubt.

Although I did not want to place Grace Paley in the position of passing judgment on her "fellow" writers, I wanted to know what she thought of the position of those who were less politically active and who often voiced during their interviews the hope that "their work would do 'it' for them," would suffice as their political involvement.

Much to my surprise, Paley the activist said, "I think it's a perfectly legitimate thing to say; I hope my work will do it for me, too. It's hard for women to talk about this because, when I'm doing a reading (and I love to have questions and answers after those, especially if I'm lucky and I can think of the answer) . . . people will sometimes say, 'Why don't you write more politics?' And I have to explain to them that writing the lives of women *is* politics. I didn't know it when I began to write; I mean I was not a feminist when I wrote my first book in 1959, but it turned out that writing about the ordinary lives of women *was* a political act, and it was a natural one for me because I was always interested in people. So when these women say, they 'hope their work will do it for them,' you know, there is no reason to think it wouldn't. Their hearts should be at rest if they are doing a lot of work. I was worried in my early days, when I wrote these stories and I didn't know if they would be made use of. I felt bad that I wasn't using my writing more politically, [although] I was writing a lot of leaflets, which is also writing, you know. Looking back, I often think that in the sixties I would have been more useful if I wrote, I don't know, manifestos, instead of hanging out on the streets so much."

While not judging other writers, Paley makes the point that she's "never been writing-ambitious the way some of the younger women are. I mean, I was always a writer, I liked being a writer, I wanted to be a writer, and when I wrote, I was a writer, and when I didn't write, I was not a writer. When I didn't write I was [a person] taking part in the political life of that period, and it was terribly exciting, you know. I was a mother and that was endlessly interesting, and it turned out to be useful to my work as well. So I see life more as a whole. The word *career* drives me crazy for some reason; I hate it in men as well as women. That word *career* is a divisive word. It's a word that divides normal life from business or professional life, whatever that is. Everybody should have work they love, that's another story, but that's different from that word *career,* which says, 'I will spend any number of hours pursuing this thing, which I may or may not be interested in even, to get somewhere, and the rest of my life is another story.' So it's a disintegrating . . . an unintegrating word. It divides a person from life, from all of life, and from their own life."

Paley says that raising children became her subject matter because "I had to get out of the house when [her two children] were little, and I spent a lot of time in the park [in New York City]. I certainly never intended for that to be what I was going to write about, because I was writing poems. I didn't know that I was coming into my community. I didn't know that I was coming into my subject matter; it was a really lucky thing for me. . . . [But] I didn't begin to write about it for several years, and had life not forced me in that direction, I don't know what would have happened. It was the luck of being pushed by circumstance into [what then became] my meat, so to speak. So I've always allowed circumstance to push me. I sometimes think it knows better what I should be doing than I do." And, she added, "It's my disposition."

In spite of her own disinclination to think about money, Paley believes that the younger women who want more power and bigger financial returns for their writing "are right. They're another generation, and . . . they should be getting what the men have been getting; there is no question about it; it's what we all have struggled for." She remembers when she "first used to send things out. Here I've said that I didn't think of myself as a feminist then, but when I sent poems out I *never* sent them out as 'Grace Paley'. I'd send them out as 'G. Paley' or 'G. G. Paley' or something like that, especially if it seemed like the poem or story had some masculine voice in it. I had brains enough to know that that would help. Well, it never helped, but I thought it did! And [now] I'm always laughing, because one of my best friends is Esther Broner, E. M. Broner, and I keep yelling at her and saying, 'Don't [send your work out as E. M. Broner] any more. Everybody knows who you are: 'It's you, Esther, it's you, Esther, it's you, Esther!" Paley laughs. "Then they'll say, 'Oh, it's *Esther* Broner; we don't want that woman.' So I appreciate what these writers are saying, and they are right."

Paley adds, however, that "I also have a politics, more of a communitarian politics. It's not to live as a poor person—I certainly don't—but it's certainly not to need so much. So I don't think about money and power issues so much. If I'm making a living, I feel okay about it, although sometimes I feel injustices at [publishing] advances." But she feels that she's older than these other writers, and, more importantly, she both writes "in a whole different way and probably lives differently as a writer. My husband probably lives more like [the other writers]—he gets up at five in the morning and writes for two or three hours before he does anything else—and he does a lot of other things and lots of politics, and he is rather exemplary. But I can't do that. I just never got in the habit. That's really one of the problems. So I don't have an inner drive to do as well as anybody else—let's put it that way. I have a great pleasure in writing and part of that is political and part of that is I'm surprised that I've done as well as I have. I really am just surprised."

Paley acknowledges that "any writer wants [the money], but then you think of how evil the whole damn thing is, and you think of others. I mean Bob has this book that came out from Johns Hopkins University Press, and I don't believe he has $150 in his promotional budget. And I spend a lot of time with other women whose advertising budgets are so low that your tendency is to want to give them half of yours, if it exists. But I understand the problem," Paley says. "It's undignified to know that some people get so much money coming their way, and although

I have fought on those issues, I never get into it on a personal basis."

Even so, "when we had this big fight at the PEN conference and tried to set up the Women's Committee, I fought those guys down to the wall, and I continue to do so, but for me that's a very political act. The fight was about this great international conference, . . . and I was in opposition to much of it, although I had the best time! You also have to have a good time at whatever you do; it's not worth struggling if you're going to be miserable. . . . You've got to fight with pleasure, if you know what I mean." And it was a pleasure, no doubt, to fight with her fellow PEN members about a poetry reading that consisted of ten men and only one woman. "I was on the PEN board, so I was really, in a sense, right in the middle of it. Those things have to be fought, wherever they are!

"But," repeated Paley, "I can't think of it personally; I just don't have the habit of thinking of it personally. And when I say the word *habit,* I really mean it; I don't mean it as a moral statement. It's not just that I've been a political person. I've been a political person who has worked with people. I've never, not from my earliest times, not been part of a group that sat and argued and fought and beat out a statement. . . . I've been part of the peace movement and gone to meetings that lasted until three in the morning. So I'm not used to thinking, 'I'm not getting this, or I'm not getting that,' especially since I feel lucky to begin with! My habit is one of turning to four or five other women and saying, 'We have to really work this out because this and this is happening.' " And she added pointedly, "In my life, I've done a lot of the things I've wanted to do outside of writing. I've had kids, and they're healthy, I married two men that I liked a lot, each one of them worth living with a long time."

When she was younger, Paley "did not live a writer's life or live among writers, hang out with them, talk about literature morning, noon, and night, all that sort of stuff. I really tried to stay away from writers for many years and was almost successful until Don Barthelme moved across the street, and we became friends, and I was sort of dragged in. I mean, I was not unfriendly to them, but there was no reason for me to hang out with them. When I was doing antiwar work and I'd go after writers for signatures, they really didn't know I was a writer anyway cause I wasn't that well known—although my first book was out. But now, of course, I know almost anybody. It's hard not to know them because I'd have to put more energy into not knowing them than it's worth."

Paley recalled with obvious sadness several friends, now deceased, who were both political people and writers. "Muriel Rukeyser was always a political person and a sad loss for some of us—for all of us, but particularly for those who knew her. She was a total poet, totally involved in literature, and she took a beating as a woman and as a poet who was not part of the elite that began to develop after the forties knocked the thirties on their head. She and somebody like Meridel Le Sueur were doubly wounded. They were wounded as women by their own political men—something like black women are—and wounded again by the literary elite, who were for the birds. But on the other hand Muriel lived very deeply in literature and with literary people. She knew them from an early age; she was close to Mexican poets, American poets, and she was political at the same time. When she got to be president of PEN she went to Korea even though she could hardly walk by then; she was very brave. [Rukeyser died of a heart attack in 1980.] So there *are* people who manage to do the whole thing." Paley talked, too, about "Kay Boyle, who from a very early age had lovers, and married, but was a writer first, second, third, sixth, and foremost. And yet on the other hand, she had six children, so you can't tell me she was a writer morning, noon, and night. . . . I just received a brand new collection of her poems, and it has her whole interesting [writer's] life in it, yet she had that whole other life too."

Since sexual harassment was very much in the news at the time of this interview, I asked Paley what she thought the writer's role was in that conflict. "The only responsibility that I can think of is that the writer has to tell the truth as she or he knows it. What a writer is, really, is someone who tells the truth in the language of the country, and sustains that language, and invigorates that language, . . . and keeps lighting up what isn't known. That's why, when new people come along, they speak a little bit differently and they enhance and make more beautiful the language. So you have black speech coming in, and our own people [the Jews] came and did something with the English language and gave it a little *schtuuup* here and there . . . and shook it up a little. Women are new people, so they come in with new subject matter," and although writers may not want to be "in charge of justice or anything like that, to some extent they are if they really are illuminating what isn't seen."

Paley, for one, is not concerned by criticism of the results of her search for illumination. Her response is, "Well, I did it the best I could. If I fucked up, someone will tell me. . . . If you screw up, someone will tell you; you don't have to worry about that! The point is never to censor yourself beforehand, but to do the most truthful thing you can. People tell me, [for instance,] 'You really should be writing about gay women because you're so close to them, and you're friends with them' and everything like that, but, on the other hand, 'You shouldn't because you're not a gay woman.' And I say, 'Well, when I'm ready to write it, I'll write it, cause it'll be my way of telling the truth."

Paley also told me that she had talked about writing to "a bunch of black kids at James Monroe High School [in New York City]. I said, 'That's your job. You have to light up the life of your people. . . . That's what you'll do naturally, and if you don't it's because you were stopped in some way. But you'll do it, and all of us will look at it and say, 'This is new, this is what we haven't seen before. Do it in your own language and that will make the general language more beautiful and truer and it will include you in it.' So the job of a writer is to aim for the truth. First of all, if you're really interested in writing, you're not going to write about what's been written about a million times, or you're not going to do it in the same old way. You can't, cause you don't know how, number one. Number two, you're not interested. You're probably becoming a writer because you're interested in trying to understand something about the world that you don't know. And, if you're truthful and you love the language, and if you are interested in society and the people, you will probably write well."

Paley reminded me that people often ask her, " 'Are you a woman writer?' I say 'Yes; I am a woman writer.' That's what I am. I'm Jewish too, a 'Jewish woman writer,' and whatever I am, I am. I don't deny any part of it. And I'm terrifically interested in what the young Chinese are writing in this country. I loved Gish Jen's book [Typical American]. She made such wonderful solutions to the language. And "I'm glad [the new Chinese-American, Japanese-American, Native American, and African-American writers] are writing about their own experiences. They have to do it. I mean, all these people feel like shit, so they have to. They're the new people, shining a light on what to them is hidden from the rest of the world; the world doesn't know what this Chinese life is," for instance, so "they are telling it to us. And I don't see how it can be avoided, that's the other thing. I don't know what else they're supposed to write about if not these immigrant stories. The Native Americans have to tell their story. . . . They are not going to tell your story, they are not going to tell mine. They can't. If they are truthful, they have to tell theirs." Paley noted that "people have been telling the Italian story for them for so long, the Italians ought to be really pissed." But, she added, if the new writers become too hateful toward other segments of the population, "then I say, 'Fuck em.' When they are hateful towards other peoples, then that's another story entirely."

Since Paley's new book is about rural life reflected in poems, "mostly about flowers," I asked her if she was returning to her original role as a writer. "No, it's just lucky someone wants to print them now. I always kept writing poetry, but I never pushed the printing of my poems or did much with them. I just had them in too many places—pages here and pages there, not organized. Years before I wrote the stories I sent out a lot of poems and none were bought except for two or three when I was about twenty. For the next twelve years or so I kept writing, but I stopped sending them out. When I began to write stories and they were finally collected in a book, that became my major thing and I felt I did stories better." She never became a novelist, Paley says, "because I *think* short stories and that seems to be it." After writing poems, she was comfortable writing short stories. "I was accustomed to completion. When I wrote my first stories I naturally had to make myself finish to know that I had written a whole prose piece, for God's sake. I was accustomed to finishing, so I wrote one, I wrote another, and pretty soon I was writing them all." Paley laughed and said, "A lot of these things are not so deep!"

She admits that she finally began to understand what was wrong with the early poems. "I loved literature even though I was crazy in the street and everything else, and the poems were a little too literary. Now they aren't. And I didn't have my own voice for poems. I did in the stories, and what began to happen was that some of that ease moved into the poems. Anyway, I never would have published them if one of my students, a woman who was a poet, hadn't had a printing press. She said, 'Can I go through your drawers and your piles of stuff?' and she put the collection together and I thought she was going to make a little chapbook, but it became a large poem book. . . . [But] right now I'm dying to get back to stories. . . . I just have to get a time distance from what I'm writing about."

This partly accounts for why Grace Paley only has "three books in print. If I had ten books, if I did a book every other year, I'd make a living." But then you recall that Paley is working "with the organizers of a group called Jewish Women against the Occupation and another one called Jews for Racial and Economic Justice" because "if you go to Israel you can't help but be very interested in Jewish affairs. I go to temple, which I don't do in New York at all, . . . and I sort of keep in touch with the Jewish community here. I mean, I have poems about being Jewish; I like being Jewish. I attribute it to the fact that even though my father was insanely antireligious, my parents never disliked Jews or being Jewish. There was never that certain kind of anti-Semitism that Jews sometimes have."

Paley added that her daughter, who lives in Vermont, realizes that there's "a general anti-Semitism which exists in the country that is not vicious, but it's sort of like a low-grade cold. You know, like everybody has it and passes it on to the children. She's often subjected to unimportant anti-Semitic remarks—not all of them virulent, but all of them painful—not like a knife in the back, but more like pins in the *tuchas*. So she thinks about that."

But in no way does it stem the flow of life that surges through the world of Grace Paley. Just as we are ready for another harrowing drive to the bus station, Paley's stepdaughter, Lisa, walks in:

"Can I borrow Dad's typewriter? I have to fill out a form and I can't do it on my computer, and no one else in town seems to *have* a typewriter!"

" 'You can use mine, darling.'

"The baby took a bottle today with milk in it!'

"Good. So you can leave her here now."

The myriad fans of Grace Paley may have a long wait for the next book.

BOOKS BY GRACE PALEY

SHORT STORIES

The Little Disturbances of Man. New York: Doubleday, 1959; Meridian, 1960; Viking, 1968, Penguin, 1985.

Enormous Changes at the Last Minute. New York: Farrar, Straus & Giroux, 1974.

Later the Same Day. New York: Farrar, Straus & Giroux, 1985;
  Penguin, 1986.

POETRY

Leaning Forward. Penobscot, Me.: Granite Press, 1985.
[with Vera Williams] *Long Walks and Intimate Talks.* New York:
  The Feminist Press, 1991.
New and Collected Poems. Gardiner, Me.: Tilbury House, 1992.
  (*Begin Again Long Ago,* audio version)

CALENDARS

[with Vera Williams] *Calendar for War Resister's League,* 1989.

Gish Jen

IN THE midst of the considerable flurry over the publication of her first novel, *Typical American,* Gish Jen is home for the weekend from Cambridge, Massachusetts, to see her parents in the big, welcoming house in the town where she went to high school. And when the door opens in Scarsdale, New York, the pregnant, curly-haired, and brainy Chinese-American writer, dressed in white cutoffs and her husband's shirt, greets you with a welcoming smile.

Gish Jen is fun. She's one of those midthirties women with a Harvard B.A., a degree from the well-respected Iowa Writers' Workshop, and a stint at Stanford Business School, who can still be described as mischievous, whether she is teasing her very correct Chinese-born mother about the absence of herb tea in the kitchen or laughing about her name: "My husband's last name is O'Connor. We thought about using Jen-O'Connor, but it kind of sounds like Jack-O-Lantern."

While they await the baby, Gish Jen has been spending part of her time promoting her novel, which *Publishers Weekly* called "a darkly humorous account of Chinese immigrants encountering America." As she explained on the PBS program "Bookmark," this is decidedly *not* the typical immigrant story where the "tired and poor" reach the paved-with-gold streets and proceed to turn into Americans at the expense of their ethnic pride or racial identity and its more familiar folkways. *Typical American* is, instead, a novel about attaining the American dream of material success, as it existed in 1947, and almost losing yourself while doing it. It traces the evolution and near dissolution of Ralph (Lai Fu, "Come Fortune") Chang, a penniless recluse who has neglected to renew his visa, and his older sister Teresa, who discovers him sleeping on a park bench in New York. It is also the story of Ralph's wife, Helen, who came to America with Teresa, and of a fully Americanized trickster figure named Grover Ding, whose name was important because "Grover sounded like Rover, which sounded like a dog's name." (Ding was created with Melville's *Confidence Man* in mind, and he has the trustability of a mangy, unloved dog and the morals of a three-card monte player who makes a living cheating tourists on New York's 42d Street.)

The novel took four years to complete. Life, as they say, intervened. Between her graduation from Harvard, and her decision to drop out of Stanford Business School, where she "read fifty novels in one year and actually spent more of my time in writing courses," Gish Jen was in fact making peace with her decision to write. It seemed from our conversation that the most difficult problem for Jen to master as she evolved into a writer was not technique or craft. Rather, she was still resisting the lifelong parental pressure to become a doctor or a lawyer and to succeed in a more economically secure field than writing. (One sister is a doctor; her three brothers are businessmen.) Most parents of first generation Americans, and particularly her Chinese-born parents (who were stranded in America when the island of Formosa fell to the Communists), would share this dream for their children.

The process of becoming a writer started at Harvard. (Jen was accepted at Yale, too, but "who wanted to go to New Haven? Boston was a fun town . . . and close to the ski areas. New Haven was ugly and dangerous. Looking back, I realize that if I'd been more serious about English, I should have gone to Yale.") A poetry class with Robert Fitzgerald turned her into a full-blown English major. "I thought, 'Finally, I am going to find out why some things are in verse.' . . . He said there would be weekly assignments. I thought he meant there'd be papers, but it turned out the weekly assignments were in verse. You had to write poems, which I couldn't believe. But I loved it, and that's really where I began writing. I said to my roommate, 'I'd love to be a poet; too bad it's so impractical'—that was the Chinese part of me speaking. That class was really where I got the bug. Fitzgerald encouraged me and said, 'You really should think about doing something in literature,' and then somebody got me a job in publishing [eighteen months working at Doubleday immediately after college], which felt really good."

But it was Jen's time in China, after she left Stanford and before she attended the Iowa writing program, that enriched her interior life and proved most helpful in her evolution. She was at loose ends when what she calls "serendipity" intervened. "I happened to have dinner with this friend of mine, who had just come back from China. Although he had relatives (particularly an uncle in a coal mining institute) who begged him to stay and teach English," he was returning to New York. "This uncle was desperate for someone to call, . . . so I said, 'Well, when does he want somebody?' And he said, 'I think he'd want somebody right now,' and I said, 'Well, I think I'll go.' So I just sort of picked up and left. We started classes as soon as they could get students there—which took some time because some of them came from inner China, and it was like a ten-day trip by train."

During that year in China, Gish Jen, the almost-writer, "first began to sort out what was Asian, what was Asian-American, and what was American." She realized that part of her struggle was not familial, but cultural. "It began," she explained, "to seem very much clearer," because when she was actually living in China, she could see that the Chinese "had characteristics in their thinking that were just like your mother's: for instance, their attitudes toward authority." She realized that when Americans think that "something is amiss with the world, they are indignant. They say, 'I'm going to go fix this; this is not right.' And the Chinese say, 'That's the way the world is; you just make your way around it without confronting it.'" Her parents had retained these ideas about confrontation and, says Jen, "they would very much discourage us if we were unhappy and we wanted to challenge authority. They thought, 'What is the matter with my child?'" She began, too, to understand the implications of "the questions they would ask: 'Do you like sweet food or do you like salty food?' That was a whole axis that my parents thought about; they liked to find out what people liked to eat. Like my parents would say, 'Oh, *this* is your favorite dish' and I would say, 'Oh, well, I like it.' . . . When I would come home from college, my mother would say 'Oh, I made this for you; this is your favorite dish.' I realized that you were supposed to have a favorite dish and [that kind of specificity and definiteness] was sort of an Asian or . . . a Chinese idea."

Jen began to understand that this kind of thinking was not so much about food, but about "the idea of ranking. I don't know if all Asian cultures have this," but in China when you're in the city they'll say, 'This is the Number One most beautiful spot' and then 'There's the Number Two.' Everything is ranked. In America we study statistics and we know that in fact the first five ranking places [on any list] are all the same really; statistically, there's no difference, right? But the Chinese love [to apply these rankings.] 'This child is Number One in the class; this is Number Two in the class.' And I really recognized my parents in this when they said, 'So, are you Number One in your class?' I can just see my father thinking that way."

She began to comprehend that "these are all strands of my parents which come from China, and they share this with all these other people. It's not just *them,* and *then you begin to understand*. And I also realized that some of what is in them has crossed over into me, like the emphasis on school and education and degrees. It was very difficult for me to leave Stanford Business School, for instance, because I didn't get a degree, and I also thought, 'Why not get this degree?' I'm sure I was admitted to give the class *diversity,* and I'm sure they'll never admit anybody like me again, and for the next ten years the admissions committee will say, 'Do you remember we admitted that Gish Jen person?' "

She has also come to feel "that Asians in general, or Chinese in general, are (or were) a feminine culture. . . . They like to stay home." Of course many feminists would be quick to point out that what Jen is calling "feminine" in this context does not inhere in the culture, but is derived from patriarchy, Asian or otherwise. But Jen says that in a novel about Chinese-Americans, "if there's a house, then there is a wall (forget about a moat) between them and the outside world. The ideal is to stay inside and to never have to go out, and the whole idea of staying home is really important. I think men do go out, but it is not glamorized the way it is here in America, where the big story is to ride out and go someplace and to travel." As she writes in *Typical American,* "the way Americans in general like to move around, the Chinese love to hold still; removal is a fall and an exile."

These ideas also surface in the novel when Helen, newly converted to American "values," falls in love with the suburbs with its "double garage with separate entrance. Finished basement. Sliding glass doors . . . breakfast nook with built-in benches . . . wall unit . . . extras galore. When Helen finally has to leave the house [to go to work], she's having *to leave the house!*" Jen says, and she is clearly traumatized.

Jen says that when Americans think about Helen's response to staying at home, they "see it as a sense of confinement, which is bad, and they would like her to have more space. But Helen is trying to make a world of her own, in a world that is very small. And the only way she has to do that is to make a space between the men." Helen, Jen insists, "would see [staying home] as great, and to go out as bad."

This insight into one of her own characters, for instance, helped Jen to understand "one of the biggest differences between me and my mother, because I did a lot of traveling. Every opportunity I had, I would go someplace, and my mother couldn't believe it. She had this daughter with wanderlust and she thought, 'What's the matter with my daughter? She always wants to *go* someplace.' And that's a big cultural thing, and it's one of the ways you can see I'm an American, and although my mother's a naturalized American, she's not as American as I am."

Perhaps this is why Helen was "the last character in the book to develop. You can see that she enters quite late, and I had the most trouble inventing her. It took me the longest time and I remember writing endless little essays to myself about who she was. I'd sit down every day and say, 'Who's Helen? Who's Helen? What is she like?' and I just couldn't get a handle on her." Jen realized that she had created a character who is caught between her husband Ralph, who has jettisoned his career as a Ph.D. in engineering at Columbia University for a quick buck as the king of a fried Chicken Palace, and the manipulator of these franchises, Grover Ding, who seduces Helen and causes Teresa to leave the family home. Ding, she says, "represents a kind of American, particularly the kind who grew up on the frontier with the Wild West ideas that are so different from Eastern establishment ideas. He epitomizes validity gone wild, and he is completely without a sense of responsibility or social structure. Ding is the opposite of the other characters who are defined by their duties." Jen explained that not all of the characters were conceived together. "Ralph and Teresa came early. Ralph came first and Teresa came second, in terms of my understanding them as characters."

It's interesting, too, that the protagonist is a man. Jen said she "anticipated that people were going to ask that all the time: 'Why do you have a male protagonist?' " The answer is, "I don't know, although it is true that you're always looking for that good protagonist to drive the narrative. You are looking for a relatively active person, and it is true that when I think of Asian-American women of that generation, I don't see them as having that robustness of narrative. . . . It's not that they have no power, but they don't tend to have eventful lives. They are more reactors, a lot of them, but not all of them." She recalled a character named Janis, Old Chao's wife, "who is out there doing things. She had more reason to change and become an American because she was less satisfied with the Old World identity. But, besides that, I really don't know why."

In fact, Gish Jen says that when she's asked to analyze too much she's "always reminded of that ditty about 'the goose that laid the golden egg, who died from looking up its crotch. If you'd lay as well, don't watch.' . . . I'd hate to take the novel apart too much because it destroys your ability to work; you become too conscious of, 'Is this interesting? Are things happening?' "

Gish Jen is also prepared for the inevitable comparisons with Amy Tan, the Chinese-American author of *The Joy Luck Club,* which sold over 425,000 hardcover copies in 1990 and whose second novel, *The Kitchen God's Wife,* jumped to first place on the *New York Times* list shortly after publication. Jen says that she hopes "we won't be lumped together," but if that happens, she will react with "a certain amount of ironic distance" because "it's a useful category up to a point." She seemed particularly intrigued to realize that people will talk to her about Amy Tan all the time. "Here are two people from relatively similar backgrounds, and it's amazing what different things we made of that." Asian-Americans do "have shared material up to a point," she acknowledged, but "two obviously different products emerged. And I guess the comparison gives [the readers] insight not only into the process, but into how much transformation is involved."

This kind of "lumping together" is exactly what Gish Jen would call "typical American," and I asked her why she thought it occurred. She thinks it is "because [America is] such a disparate culture that there's an inherent problem in knowing what *is* American—whereas if you're Chinese, you know very definitely what that means. Here we don't know, so, as we struggle to answer that question, it comes down to, 'We're *not* this.' That's the simplest way: a 'not-this' culture, because there's no other way to answer the question. Actually, I think there are other ways [to answer this question.] For instance, we can say that Americans are preoccupied with the question 'Who am I?' which is a question we ask all the time, and other cultures don't." In the novel, one of the characters "started out as Chinese. And, by the time he's asking that question—'Who am I?'—he's American. He's crossed some kind of line; it's not a question he would ever have asked before."

Gish Jen's writing style is distinguished by a practical, ungilded approach to reality: She does not soften the hard edges of experience for her characters or her readers. But she seems to revel in the critical opinion that she "pushes things to the edge and that there is more of an edge to my work." This is what A. G. Mojtabai was referring to in the *New York Times* when she wrote that "there's no pause, no underlining, no winking aside to the reader to signal how clever this is, how humorous that is. The author just keeps coming at you, line after stunning line." Jen insists, in fact, that "as a writer, I thought very hard about things in my writing that were *nice*. I endeavored not to be nice and to try to be a little tougher. I write to the point of danger. I write to the point . . . when I can hear my mind going off—danger, danger, danger—and I try to hold with it and not just back away.

"The people I seem to admire are the people who are even tougher than I am: Jamaica Kincaid, who I think lays it on the line; man, does she! She's so brave I just shudder, and I aspire to be like her. There are people who are a little wicked and I like wickedness. Mavis Gallant: She's a little wicked. I wouldn't want to be a friend of hers in a way; I wouldn't want to end up in any of her stories, but she's hard and she's right. . . . [Her wickedness] is not gratuitous. I think Alice Munro [has a hard edge too and] I really admire her. I admire the hell out of her."

Gish Jen's ability to follow her own course surfaced even before *Typical American* was published. "I didn't go near the publishing establishment until I was almost finished with the novel. And I did that on purpose, really. I'd seen so many people take their novels, when they're two years into the writing, to an agent; and the work looks exactly like what a novel looks like after two years. Sure enough, the agents and editors are not clairvoyant. So they'd say these ninety things about how to finish it." What happens then is that "the writers get completely depressed and are unable to finish, or they start rewriting the book in accordance with what they think the editors want. Writers get very confused, and they start to listen to these other voices, and they try to write somebody else's book, and then there's a big mess.

"This happens particularly to first novelists, and *I just didn't want this to happen to me.* So I stayed away. I got lots of letters from agents and editors because I'd been getting grants and stuff, and when you get grants, you get letters. I just put them all into one big pile. I thought, 'Okay, so I have all these names. This is great.' I would write them a letter saying, 'Thank you very much. I'll get back to you when I'm done.' And I just left the big pile there until I knew that nothing they could say was going to change what I'd written and that my direction couldn't be changed, and until I could say, 'You can take it or leave it. If you don't like it, that's too bad.' "

Gish Jen was ready for me when I asked what I thought was
my final question. I wanted to know whether she had received
pressure from her publisher, or anyone else connected with her
book, to change her Chinese-sounding first name. She was busy
trying to stifle her laughter as she said, "You know, my legal
name is Lillian. And Gish is not an Asian name. It's from Lillian
Gish. It's funny, because some people will automatically say,
when I say 'My name is Gish,' 'Oh, like Lillian Gish?' Other
people will hear 'Gish' and assume it comes from 'geisha' or
'geesh.'

"My mother used to call me 'Lily,' and when I signed her copy
of the book, I wrote, 'Love, Lil.' But in high school I always had
a lot of nicknames. My friends were sort of going into our art
phase, and I had a friend named Housman and she was [called]
'A. E.' I became Gish, but these were names we only used in a
very small circle. Then, when I was a junior in high school, I
went to this science-foundation archeology dig in Pennsylvania.
We were sitting around the circle and it was very magical; there
was a hurricane, and a building had just been hit by lightning.
. . . And they got to me and said, 'What's your name?' Just for
fun I said, 'My name's Gish, Gish Jen.' And that's the first time
everybody called me 'Gish.'

"I read all these things about writers inventing themselves,
and I think it was a way of having my own identity. It was
different from the identity I had been given by my parents. But
now I have to say that I disapprove of Lillian Gish; she's in all
those horrible movies like *Birth of a Nation,* and she's not somebody that I admire, so don't get me wrong. But I do love the
name Gish; I think it's a good time!"

Now that Gish Jen is completely committed to writing, she
has decided that she has "a very low tolerance for boredom, . . .
and I know that means," she said with her mischievous smile,
"that I have no inner resources. I don't know; there is simply a
big aspect of play in writing novels, and making the story more
and more elaborate is just more and more fun." Mostly, she
admits, "I think I'm trying to keep myself from being bored.

When I think about why I would be a writer, why I should continue to be a writer, it seems to me one of the few things you can do where you're never bored. And I *hate* being bored."

BOOKS BY GISH JEN

FICTION

Typical American. Boston: Houghton Mifflin, 1991; Plume, 1992.

Janette Turner Hospital

BECAUSE Janette Turner Hospital understands the social, sexual, and emotional price women pay in our patriarchal culture, all of her fiction, to one degree or another, deals with silence, with violence, and with what Hospital calls "the silencing of women about that violence." Much of Hospital's dynamic sensitivity is defined by the clipped, charged, one-word titles of her novels and short-story collections: *Charades, Borderline, Dislocations,* and *Isobars,* and even the longer titles, *The*

Tiger and the Tiger Pit and *The Last Magician,* immediately reflect her concerns and her angle of vision.

Although Janette Turner Hospital is "psychically, bodily" an Australian, we arrived for this interview at her rented, fourth floor, lavender and blue apartment in a brownstone near Boston University, where she teaches one semester a year. She had just returned from Kingston, Ontario, where she lives for a third of each year; the remaining time she spends in Australia where she has a continuing appointment at La Trobe University in Melbourne.

Hospital had recently been in residence at the University of Melbourne's Ormand College, where she was the first creative writer to hold the G. E. M. Scott Fellowship. "This quite extraordinary experience . . . was doubly meaningful because it was in Australia, where I had weathered the storm of being an expatriate for a couple of years. Although I was born in Melbourne, I left it when I was seven years old for Brisbane, Queensland, 1,200 miles north, which is like moving to Louisiana or Mississippi. (I grew up in the steamy, subtropics and I write about the rainforest.) I think if I'd known in advance that I was only the third woman fellow in the history of the most venerable university college in the country and that the preceding two women were Baroness Warnock, Mistress of Girton College, Cambridge, and Toril Moi, the well-known feminist critic, I would have been too intimidated to accept. I didn't realize what company I was stepping into, but for me it seemed unreal. I couldn't quite believe that this great gathering of 250 people had come to a lecture ["Cat Fights and Tomcats and Independent Women"] to hear me. And then there was a reception with over 200 people, including high court justices and the whole old-boy network at an old-boy college, and I kept thinking that I would wake up. For any writer it's a very unusual experience, because you're so used to isolation, and lots of flak, and reviews that hurt.

"And then there was this half-comic/half-bewildering pantomime of 'High Table.' The University of Melbourne is set up on the Oxford principle of university colleges, and Ormand College

is the oldest and the best endowed of these. It's very Oxfor-
dian—looking, architecturally absolutely splendid, and it's only
been coed for about five years." The enrollment is now about 50
percent women and "they have to have three sittings for dinner;
at any time there are a couple of hundred students in the dining
hall. But the middle of the three dinner sessions is the one called
'High Table,' and some of the thirty fellows—some of them res-
ident, some of them visiting fellows—would repair at precisely
6:20 P.M. to the Master's Common Room, where the Master of
the College and the Fellows would have sherry before dinner.
At 6:30 we would process into the dining room. We all wore
academic gowns, and so did the students, who have to wear
academic gowns to dinner, and they would all rise and we would
process down the aisle to sit at what was literally a high table,
since it was on a dais. I must say that the Master's Common
room was a wonderful institution because there were Fellows—
male and female, from all over the world, leading scholars in
their fields—and to be one of the group, talking to this dazzling
collection of international scholars over sherry every evening,
made me see what the old-boy network really is—incredible
connections in these scholarly fields.

"I had seen the dramatization of Virginia Woolf's *A Room of
One's Own* here at the Loeb Theatre the first week I was down
in Boston, where Woolf described watching the men's colleges
at Oxford [in 1929] and compared it to the women's college and
the dreadful little grotty meals they had there, and I thought,
'This is it! And miraculously, by some completely freakish little
accident, here I am.' At the end of the meal the Fellows and the
Master processed out and back into the senior Common Room
for port and coffee and sitting-around-the-fire conversation.

"Sitting around for conversation was wonderful. I talked mostly
to a feminist historian, Linda Ryan, who was doing research on
female convicts and Australian attitudes toward them. It was
exciting to meet someone working on that kind of thing, so we
would hole up in a corner every night and talk." At that time
Hospital was writing her latest novel, *The Last Magician,* "I was

increasingly feeling silenced, and the frightening thing was not me feeling silenced by the male power structures of society— which I sensed very powerfully during the Anita Hill hearings— but also being silenced by other women, sometimes describing themselves as strong feminists. I found this quite devastating. I was looking back for an explanation for this particular feminist stance [of defending silence], which is even more damaging to women who have experienced violence, and I think in Australia it goes right back to convict days. The women convicts were repeatedly gang raped on the ships on the way out [to Australia]. Even if they weren't, strictly speaking, sold or assigned as slaves, in practice that's what it amounted to. They were greatly out-numbered, and they were sort of portioned out for sexual release to the officers and the male convicts. The accounts one reads of the first female convicts are horrific, but they were considered by all the male convicts and the male officers to be the most degraded sluts—even though it was the women who were con-stantly, crudely, violently, and sexually abused and used.

"When the women began acting out, their behaviors were interpreted as promiscuous, especially in the diaries of male offi-cers writing back to their very pure wives in England—the wives who were contrasted constantly with these 'licentious, promis-cuous sluts,' even though these women had no control whatso-ever over the number of men who had sexual access to them. This is just the worst kind of unjust obscenity!

"When the first free women came out—and various feminist historians have written about this in Australia—they wanted to distance themselves as much as possible from the female con-victs, and no one was harsher to female convicts or more unsympathetic to the degree of violence in their lives, or more likely to condemn them as sexual marauders, than those first free women.

"I can't help but feel that that's left a long, dangerous, and damaging legacy in Australian life. When the first feminist his-torian, Miriam Dickson, did a book called *The Real Mathilda* on the identity of women in Australia, she was savagely attacked by many leading feminists because . . . she was pointing out, really, that some women did not [and do not] have control of their lives. But many feminists in Australia have bought into a stereo-type and are in effect saying, 'Victims are asking for it.' " They say that "an ideologically sound feminist must not portray a woman as victim now, because then you are in effect saying, 'If you are a victim, you are setting up a bad role model and that's improper: A good feminist is not a victim.' *But what happens to a woman who is raped, who is overpowered physically, attacked and so on?* To tell a woman who is overpowered that she must not speak of the experience of being a victim is the worst kind of double whammy, and it just silences women."

Unfortunately, this is a subject that Hospital knows from per-sonal experience since she was attacked in 1988 by four men in Boston who held a knife to her throat. She readily reveals that "there are times when I feel fairly acutely at risk of functioning. . . . When I was mugged I did flip back very badly to [previous] states of terror, so one of the themes that I have a character state in the new novel, *The Last Magician,* is that absences are crucial and that silences can speak very loudly. Noting the silenced women is to me a revolutionary act.

"I felt that particularly in wake of the criticism I got for my character, Verity, in *Charades,* which initially had a much longer title. It was going to be *A Thousand and One Confections of Cha-rade,* an obvious tipoff that this was a contemporary *Thousand and One Nights* about game-playing, multiple perspectives on Charade, guessing games, and enigmas. The theme of the book dealt with the fact that all our thought constructs and our behav-ior patterns are a kind of elaborate ritualized game, but for some people it's a very deadly game.

"That criticism broke my heart because I see Verity as an immensely strong person who fought for a very long time against the silence. [Verity Ashkenazy is a Jewish refugee from France whose parents were imprisoned in a concentration camp when she was six.] Verity fights against her trauma successfully for most of her life, but eventually is overpowered by the weight of the past. I was baffled and stunned and bewildered that *Cha-rades* was attacked by feminists as being an antifeminist novel because this woman *became* a victim *because* she was passive, *because* she was silenced. I'd been working on the book before I was attacked by the four guys who surrounded me and held a knife to my throat, and I wrote the second half of the book trying to exorcise these very deep feelings of panic and trauma."

Hospital feels that she "was sort of scrambling for personal survival in order not to become Verity, and my writing *Charades* was partly exorcising the worse-case scenario. *Charades* was attacked for the [depiction of the] struggle itself, and Verity was attacked for bearing witness to the struggle. And to be attacked by other women was really, really devastating, and I felt then [in 1989] that I didn't want to write again."

In all her novels, Hospital explained, "I am always bifurcating my women; I always have pairs." In *Borderline,* a novel about a Salvadoran's escape to Canada, "they're very clearly and allegor-ically named as two sides of the coin, Felicity [happiness] and Dolores [sadness], one who makes it, and one who doesn't, and I'm really writing about the two sides of myself." In addition, "my two closest girlfriends from high school were adult sui-cides—so I feel I'm close enough to the women who don't make it."

That's why, Hospital says, "I'm doing [it] again in *The Last Magician,* fighting against the long silence. . . . What I've ended up doing is writing about a woman who becomes psychologi-cally mute, and I realize that it is a personal statement about myself, about feeling silenced as a literary voice." Maybe, she mused, "this will wear off, maybe I will feel differently, and maybe it's just the postpartum exhaustion of finishing a book, but it's never happened to me before. The next book has always been bursting to come out before the last one is finished, and I don't know, the way I feel now, I feel that I won't write again."

The mugging in Boston also "reawakened earlier childhood traumas for me of being bullied at school as the weirdo religious child from a very strict religious family," lingering memories of

an isolating and difficult childhood and the feeling of being under
attack by both Canadians and Australians for being an expatriate. "I certainly realized that right from the beginning—even
before I moved geographically to a different country—I had
simultaneously lived in two worlds. It was not dissimilar to
growing up Mennonite or as a Hasidic Jew. But Mennonites and
Hasidic Jews usually don't go to the public schools. They keep
to themselves, and although they live in a hermetically sealed
world, it has coherence." In Hospital's case, she "felt like a space
traveler who every day traveled through a time warp from this
very secluded, Pentecostal home to a public school. It cost me
plenty, but the savagery I experienced came from teachers and
kids at school, from the intolerance to difference and the cruelty
to someone who is different.

"I have gradually extricated myself from the Church, since as
I got older it was intellectually, as well as socially, stifling. Almost
everything was forbidden. (My parents and my brothers, however—very good, simple people—are still in the Church and
very dear to me.) The Jimmy Swaggerts and the Jim Bakkers
could not be more remote from this Church. These people are
all very poor, and I realize now that the Church was the only
thing that gave dignity and validation to lives that were margin-
alized financially, socially, and every other way.

"There were close boundaries around what you could read,
what you could question, what you could do. I was twenty-one
years old before I saw a movie, and I lived an extremely protected life. But what was difficult was that each day I journeyed
to the world of Australian public school—a very macho, philistine, hedonistic male culture."

Hospital remembers her first years at school as "intense, clue-
gathering years, and it was great training for a writer. When you
are from this Pentecostal, evangelical, fundamentalist background, you are acutely conscious of language because you don't
know what things *mean*—since we had no radio (that was poverty), no TV (it didn't come to Australia until 1953, I think, and
for a long time people in the Church resisted getting it), and we

did not get a newspaper. Certainly you didn't go to movies! My parents didn't get a TV until about five years ago because it was felt that the worldly things that had been kept at bay would then come right into your living room. I remember hearing sermons preached about the devil's pipeline into the home. . . .

"There's always been a low tolerance of difference in Australia," Hospital added, "which is gradually changing as the nation is becoming a more cosmopolitan society. But then it was a WASP society. ('Anglo-Celtic' is the term of preference because it's not just Anglo-Saxon, since the Irish stream [from the convicts] is a huge segment of Australian life.) It's not at all insignificant that the true story of the mother in the Meryl Streep movie, *A Cry in the Dark,* was a huge legal case that went on for years and years. Most Australians believe she's guilty and that this woman murdered her baby; that is popular opinion. And it's not at all insignificant that she was a Seventh Day Adventist. If you are different from the mainstream, you are victimized by all kinds of folk and superstitious beliefs—that you are into Sabbaths and murdering babies—the things they used to say about the Jews, because they were different. Australia has always been like that . . . and so I was the marked kid." And ever since then, Hospital realizes, "the one thing that is really, really difficult to deal with, and I don't just mean difficult to deal with, I mean at acute psychic risk when it happens, is being singled out for a public attack."

In spite of her childhood, Janette Turner Hospital feels her Australian connection very deeply. So it was with some bitterness that she told me about the "big verb in Australia, which is *to swan in*—'Who does she think she is, having won literary prizes overseas, swanning back in, thinking she can be part of the Australian scene?' I had two years of that," she says, "and it took me to my sixth book to get a good review in the *Sydney Morning Herald.* That was painful, that really hurt, to get this flak from the literary world in Australia. And the Canadians were happy with me until I started visiting Australia," but now this kind of thing "is happening from Canada, since Canada has always treated expatriates badly."

This particular form of isolation is reflected in Hospital's first short-story collection, *islocations,* where wistful cultural outsiders like Sani, supposedly the descendant of a Moghul prince (but now a Canadian waiter) and Perpetua Engine-wallah, the Goan, half-Christian woman with whom he makes love once each year, appear. There are also the inmates of a maximum security prison and their teacher in a course on the 'prisoner as hero.' "

Isobars ("an isobar is an imaginary line connecting places of equal pressure on a map"), her second collection of stories, charts very clearly the intrusion of painful and unresolved memory into an amorphous and insecure present. Again, the characters for the most part are now Canadians, displaced on not always friendly soil and coping with the multiple losses of place, time, and identity. In one story, "Here and Now," Alison, an Australian teaching in Toronto, learns of her mother's death in Brisbane, "in the early hours of tomorrow morning" and flies home "all the way back to the beginning." And in "The Second Coming of Come-by-Chance," a submerged city resurfaces and triggers the memory of a rape that happened forty years earlier. The scars of violence against women mark many of the stories.

One should not conclude from her comments in this interview that the very blonde and petite Janette Turner Hospital projects only pain and sadness. She is happily married to Clifford Hospital ("a French Huguenot name"), a dean at Queen's University in Kingston who received his doctorate in Sanskrit texts and comparative history of religion at Harvard, and she is the mother of two children, a daughter and a son. Both children, "North American beings, the greatest ongoing joy in my life," were raised in Canada.

On the other hand, one understands quickly after talking with Hospital that she has been deeply touched by the experiences of her life and has made something valuable and true from them. To counteract adverse criticism, she is "gradually learning to put faith in a network of writers and former students. When I was back in Canada recently, I went through the mail and there was a postcard from a woman who did a writing workshop with me a few summers ago. She'd been to Paris with her husband, and she sent me a postcard to tell me that *Charades* was in the window of a famous Shakespearean bookstore there. This astonished me. So often you feel that you're not making a mark anywhere in the world. Then you're caught offguard, something happens that you'd never have imagined—your book is displayed in a Paris bookstore, especially *that* Paris bookstore!

"I'm beginning to cherish these positive moments, especially as one who, through no choice of my own, has been very nomadic, who feels she has no natural constituency, no [national] body to endorse me (although my warmest feedback does come from Australia now), and no natural readership or support group, and who sometimes feels so lonely and so isolated."

But she realizes, too, both as a multinational writer with a unique perspective, a teacher, and an activist with Amnesty International, that she is not really isolated. As she said, "A big issue for me is individual, moral, and political accountability for things that are, in most senses, beyond our power to do much about. But that doesn't let us off the hook." And in her fiction she's "looking at the issue of people who think of themselves as neutral and apolitical, because it's important to my literary projects to have characters who didn't have a particular axe to grind, but who nevertheless, and willingly, got caught up in the field of history."

An especially poignant evocation of personal accountability surfaces in a collection where twenty-six Australian writers talk about the idea of homeland. Hospital's autobiographical essay, "After Long Absence," recalls her childhood friend who "knows more than anyone I have ever met. He knows the sap of trees and their differing uses, he knows where tadpoles breed, he knows which ants bite and which don't, he knows how to read the telltale flying-fox tracks in banana clumps, and, . . . at school, he knows nothing.

"It was said," recalled Hospital, "that he tamed flying foxes and kept them as pets, it was said that he could fly, it was said that he could travel underground and pass through walls and that he had a magic protector, a guardian angel maybe, or maybe a devil, who held an invisible shield between his backside and the cane. He was bad. All the teachers and all the girls said he was bad. His name was Paddy McGee.

"For reasons unclear, one of the teachers, a rough giant of a man named Mr. Bryce, thrashes Paddy McGee to within an inch of his life, and the hushed class watches in fascinated terror as blood oozes from the purple welts on Paddy's legs. . . . 'I'll teach you, you insolent filthy little mick,' thunders Mr. Bryce." That afternoon he does not appear at the back fence, but when Hospital, here named Stella, finds him, "Paddy says, 'You wanna be my blood sister?' 'Yes,' she says. And with his pocketknife, he makes a small cut in the vein at his wrist, and then in hers, and he places his wrist against hers, flesh to flesh, blood to blood." Paddy disappears and "She never sees him again."

Then, Hospital writes, in what could be the credo of the accountable: "Who decides what is margin and what is text? Who decides where the borders of the homeland run? Absences and silences are potent. It is the eloquent margins which frame the official history of the land. As for geography, there are divisions and boundary lines that fissure any state more deeply than the moat it digs around the nationhood. In every country there are gaping holes. People fall through them and disappear. Yet on every side there are also doors to a wider place, a covert geography under sleep where all the waters meet."

BOOKS BY JANETTE TURNER HOSPITAL

NOVELS

The Ivory Swing. Toronto: McClelland & Stewart, 1982; Seal, 1983; Dutton, 1983; Bantam, 1984.

The Tiger in the Tiger Pit. Toronto: McClelland & Stewart, 1983; Seal, 1984; Dutton, 1984; Bantam, 1985.

Borderline. Sydney: Hodder & Stoughton, 1985; Toronto: McClelland & Stewart, 1985; Seal, 1986; Dutton, 1985; Bantam, 1986; Virago, 1990.

Charades. St. Lucia, Queensland, Australia: University of Queensland Press, 1988.

The Last Magician. New York: Holt, 1992.

SHORT STORIES

Dislocations. Toronto: McClelland & Stewart, 1986; Norton, 1990.

Isobars. Toronto: McClelland & Stewart, 1991; Baton Rouge: Louisiana State University Press, 1991; Virago, 1992.

MYSTERIES

As Alex Juniper

A Very Proper Death Melbourne: Penguin, 1990; Toronto: Random House, 1990, 1991; Scribners, 1991; Virago, 1992.

Margot Livesey

WHEN you are sitting at eleven o'clock in the morning with Margot Livesey in the empty, brick-walled cocktail lounge of the City University's Graduate Center on New York's 42d Street, it's hard to imagine that this gentle, soft-spoken Scotswoman "grew up sort of in a field. There was nothing around except boys and sheep. And lots of heather. My father taught in a boy's public school, by which, of course, I mean a private school, that was way out in the country, about fifty miles north of Edinburgh, near Perth, which was our nearest town."

When Livesey finally left that idyllic spot, she went to the University of York for a B.A. in English and philosophy and "spent seven or eight years traveling around Europe and Canada." Gradually, she said, her "stories started getting published in Canadian magazines, and that's why *Learning By Heart* [a collection of stories] was published in Canada first. Then it dawned on me that one could get jobs in American universities simply on the strength of publications, and that's what I started doing" at Rutgers, the University of Washington in Seattle, Tufts, Carnegie Mellon, and Williams. She has recently been in residence at the Iowa Writers' Workshop, a place, she says, with "so many siloes, so many cornfields, so much sky."

It's both ironic and wonderful that Livesey is now writing stories and novels where the main character is often a child. Although she is only in her late thirties, she has "the sort of ambiguous gift of being an orphan, which in some ways as a writer is very useful, although, of course, in some ways, it's very distressing." Because she does not have brothers or sisters either, she "has relatively few people to answer to," and therefore she has "kind of copyrighted certain characters."

All of Livesey's fictional children are what might be called marvelous deviants, full of a kind of familiar evil that is both innocuous and powerful. The character of Jenny, who dominates her first novel, *Homework,* is a case in point. She is one of the many motherless children who are scattered throughout contemporary fiction. (In this case, her parents are divorced and her mother is, in effect, absent from the child's life.) But Jenny is also the daughter of Stephen, who shares a house with Celia, a "thirty-something editor of education texts who has escaped the pain of an unfaithful lover by leaving London and moving to Edinburgh." The plot itself evolved from a letter, written by the mother of a daughter who was terrorizing the entire household, that Livesey read in a newspaper. In a similar fashion,

Celia and Stephen quickly become the victims of an "increasingly sinister" Jenny, who cuts a hole in Celia's new sweater, tortures a pet rabbit, steals money from Celia's purse, leaves a decomposing mouse in the bureau drawer, and finagles Stephen into a game of hide and seek during which Celia is nearly stranded on an island as the tide is coming in.

Stephen, who has the familiar denial mechanisms associated with a guilty and doting father, is oblivious to the mounting pile of childhood transgressions, and he, in effect, further isolates Celia "on the path to an irreversible conflagration." In spite of all this, Livesey said that "I certainly don't think of, and didn't particularly want the reader to think of, Jenny as evil. I think that she has very strong desires, and she goes much further than most people would to get what she wants, but it was also important to me to suggest the ways in which her father's live-in girlfriend comes to understand her and not to see Jenny as just a kind of Iago character acting malevolently for no motive. She has motives: You may not agree with them, but we can recognize them." The larger issue of Jenny's continuing malevolence, and of what Celia can do about its power over her own life, is not resolved. This is the unwritten chapter, and the reader is left with a number of questions. Livesey says, "There is no solution except for Celia to walk away. That seems to be the only solution because you can't get rid of the child." And "that's why a child is a much more fatal adversary than another woman. I suppose, in a way, that Celia recognizes Jenny's rights. She remembers the pain of her own childhood, and in some ways she recognizes that Jenny has a right to her father" because Celia, too, is a kind of motherless child in a woman's body, and Jenny's experience, Livesey admits, is supposed to resonate in Celia.

Celia is a passive character who most American readers, especially women, would probably like to send to assertiveness training class. Livesey laughed when she said that "several other people [have] commented on that. I think it is partly a national difference. I do think the British are less likely to raise their voices and . . . to confront situations in an explicit way. I also think that there is a certain kind of double vision. Many women who read the book commented on the way Celia put up, for instance, with Louis [her previous boyfriend in London], but her relationship with Louis was just born from my friends. I didn't have to make up one thing about that relationship! It was so true to life, and yet, of course, no woman actually wants to read about a woman who endures a relationship where she puts up with so much grief from a man. We don't like to see ourselves in print in certain ways, and I think that, similarly, people don't like characters in novels to be passive even though in real life we may often endure impossible situations."

As Francine Prose has written, the plot of *Homework* in part echoes Henry James's *The Turn of the Screw* "in its willingness to illuminate the dark side of childhood." Livesey said that she was "actually very pleased with this comparison. There were certain books that I was looking over my shoulder at while I was writing *Homework,* and certainly *The Turn of the Screw* was one of them. I was interested in the ambiguity that James managed to create and maintain, the sense that everything is always in question and that the nature and the spirit of children are most in question: how much they know and how deeply implicated they are. That was a fascinating part of the novel to me, so I was gratified that someone who wasn't aware of my fascination should pick that up from reading it."

Livesey explained that, "like many writers, I'm aware that romantic territory is very well trodden at the moment" and that she has deliberately chosen to examine the pain and the power of childhood. "One of the things I was always conscious of as a child, and I remain conscious of it as an adult who knows children, is that children occupy very much their own world, which in many ways is quite separate from the adult world: different preoccupations and different priorities. Adults are important to the child's world, but they are perhaps not as important as adults like to think they are."

She agreed that adults are important for setting boundaries, which the children then spend a lot of time trying to circumvent. "So I'm very intrigued by that world of childhood and by the sort of double standard to which children are subjected. I think, on the one hand, . . . that childhood memories are the most vivid and that most of us have childhood memories which govern a whole gamut of emotions and feelings and thoughts"; on the other hand, "in our dealings with children it's uncomfortable to acknowledge that a child has such a range of desires. So I think we tend to oversimplify children. It's too unpleasant," for instance, "if we really think that Johnny doesn't want to move from Nebraska to Maine. Johnny just has to move from Nebraska to Maine because he's only ten, and his wishes don't count." A novel like *Homework* reminds us that the emotions of hostility and anger we felt as children remain hard to assuage, and with Livesey we experience them once more in print.

Livesey is now finishing a second novel called *Eva Moves the Furniture,* which is "loosely based on the fact that my mother, who died [in 1956] at age thirty-six (which at one point seemed very old to me and now seems no age at all), had a kind of sixth sense. She saw poltergeists. Everything I know about my mother is in the novel, but it's a very small number of facts." What Livesey has for material are those facts associated with her mother's life, but not the emotional content for which she has been searching, and she admits that "it's disconcerting to run into a kind of wall every place you go. Her name was Eva, [which is] a beautiful name and seems right for the character." Livesey said that she herself makes a brief appearance [in *Eva Moves the Furniture*]. "I only get to be two years old, and I am a rambunctious, troublesome child called Ruth, a name that was very intentionally selected, since I often do choose names very carefully and very intentionally. I chose Ruth not so much because of Ruth's devotion to Naomi, but because I associate the name with sorrow and exile, and the word *rue,* and didn't Ruth shed tears amid the alien corn?" She felt that it was "too distracting to use my own name, although Joan Didion does it in *Democracy* and Philip Roth does it." This is "especially [true] because it's late in *[Eva Moves the Furniture],* and it seemed like an intrusion."

She laughingly said, "it sounds like I'm writing nothing but autobiographies," when she explained that she is now also working on a novel about her father (who died at the age of seventy-one in 1975), which is tentatively called *A Confirmed Bachelor.* "I had the illusion that one could just find out about an ordinary person, since I had read Richard Ellmann's biography of Oscar Wilde, and an amazing amount is known about Wilde. So I thought, 'Well, my father died fairly recently, I can find out about him,' but in actual fact what I discovered after eighteen months of searching is that I simply can't. He left no records, didn't write letters," and, as he aged, "he became more and more reclusive, and more and more of his friends were around his age." He did remarry after the death of Livesey's mother, but his second wife also died in the early 1980s. In order to research *A Confirmed Bachelor* she started to interview "people who knew him, but I broadened this because there were not a whole lot of those people left." Now she has started to reconstruct or to reinvent his life by interviewing "people who lived parallel lives to his, who went to Cambridge University or who are sufficiently elderly." A gentle, thoughtful, but saddened Margot Livesey looked up and said, "It's astonishingly hard to find out about him, and it's a real lesson in how quickly people disappear."

This novel will be set during the period from 1904 to 1945, which Livesey thinks "is the most fascinating period of British history," a revolutionary period "in . . . family life, public life, and political life." And although she has not been able to uncover the details of her own father's life, she has "become addicted to finding out about the life of the century. In a few years—even now—there will be very few people around who were born under Queen Victoria, who remember the Edwardian age with its absurdly high hopes and its enormous class divisions, its huge empire on which the sun never set, who remember the onslaught of the First World War and the way people went off to that war and disappeared and never came back." She wants to listen to the people "who remember the kind of struggles of the twenties when class warfare erupted in a way that it hadn't in quite a number of years in Britain, in order to bring together the political and the private life in the way Rosellen Brown does in *Civil Wars*.

"All of those things are fading into the past, and to find people who experienced them in some small way has become in itself a fascinating project to me." She has found those people by advertising in local newspapers and by writing letters to "various local papers. My father worked mostly in these public schools or public universities, and they keep very good records of alumni. So it's actually possible to find every person who went to his school or his university, who is still alive. I wrote a kind of form letter and then when people responded, it became more personal. And those people would sometimes put me in touch with other people, and people who hear about my project suggest other people."

Livesey's ideal interviewee is "over eighty," and even though the distance between the event and the present is very great, Livesey thinks the memories are still viable. In fact, she believes that "the past is just as unfixed and fluctuating as the future. The past is constantly subjected to change. Certainly one sees that clearly in love affairs, where people have one view of history while the affair is in progress, and may have another view after it has ended. I think that kind of revision of the past is a continual part of our history."

Livesey's elderly subjects "do have a different perspective from that of a younger interviewee, but sometimes it's a reassuring perspective. They will say, for instance, about the [then] present [Thatcher] regime in Britain, that it reminds them of what things were like under Balfour or under Macmillan. They will look back thirty or forty years and find an apt comparison. They do remind you that things change, and there is something very reassuring about that." And most of them, surprisingly, "became completely used to the idea of a woman prime minister, and some of them even said that Margaret Thatcher could do no wrong, although there are now fewer and fewer of those." Some of these elderly Etonians "are very radical. They look back to the great days of socialism and they say that before socialism came in life was hard, . . . and it's terrible to see it being dismantled."

Perhaps, she added, "one of the reasons that I write is to make something that will last a little longer, to hold on to things. It is disturbing to realize how little you can know of . . . your parents. I did live with my father for eighteen years and yet I know so little of his life, maybe because he was over fifty when I was born and seemed older, remote." As with *Eva Moves the Furniture,* the novel about her mother, Livesey regrets that once again she is running "into a kind of wall every place I go."

Margot Livesey is acutely aware of the many ways in which her stories depend on the often missing details of her own life and the transitory quality of experience. I found it interesting, for instance, that even her Scottish accent had disappeared, but she said that she had "never really had one" and had "always sounded more or less like this. My parents were both part English and most of the people at the school were from Oxford or Cambridge and had very English kinds of accents. . . . I grew up thinking that the local accent was 'common.' That was what my parents thought, and certainly if I had come home using it they would have said, 'Don't say that. Don't talk that way.' "

In spite of Livesey's considerable losses, she understands, as do all the best writers, how even sketchy memories energize fiction. In the tradition of James Joyce, who looked back at Dublin from his home in Zurich, and of Proust, who examined his memories from Paris, we can look forward to more novels from this fine and acutely sensitive writer as she looks back at her northern home in Scotland from whichever American college is fortunate enough to hire her.

Margot Livesey

BOOKS BY MARGOT LIVESEY

NOVELS

Homework: New York: Viking, 1990; Penguin, 1991.

SHORT STORIES

Learning by Heart. Ontario: Penguin, 1986; New York: Penguin, 1987.

TEXTBOOKS

[with Lynn Klamkin] *Writing About Literature*. New York: Holt, Rinehart, 1986.

Connie Porter

CONNIE PORTER may not be "putting on the Ritz," but she had her first cup of imported tea there recently among the most proper of Bostonians, as the harpist played in the background. It was only one day in the life of a young writer who is having a very good time and with good reason.

Her first book, *All-Bright Court,* was bought by a major publisher; she has a powerful New York agent ("a hard worker"); the novel was selected by the Book-of-the-Month Club; the paperback rights, as they say in publishing, "went to auction"; she was offered a full-time, tenure-track, teaching job at Southern Illinois University; she has a new red Toyota with black leather bucket seats; and she was leaving soon for an eight-city tour from Seattle to Buffalo to talk about her novel. No wonder this thirty-one-year old writer from western New York state is excited. "I grew up as one of nine kids living in a housing project and going to public school and all that, so I'm not familiar with the publishing process, but from what I can understand, it's rare for the Book-of-the-Month Club to take on a first novel, especially from someone unheard of. It's not as if I had published short stories in seventeen *New Yorkers* and I'm a household name. I feel really honored that so many people have decided to take a chance on me."

All-Bright Court was first written as a twelve-page short story in a class at Louisiana State University where Connie Porter was studying for a master's in fine arts. When she was at the Bread Loaf Writers' Conference one summer, a well-known New York writer read the story and introduced Porter to her agent. The agent sold the expanded story to Houghton Mifflin. "When they bought the book it was 167 pages long, and, naive as I was, I just said, *'Here it is. This is my book,'* and they said, 'Wonderful. Do you think you can double it?' I said, *'Double it?'* But they were really patient." It was two years before the book was actually finished. "They saw some promise there, and they took it on as it was, with the contract stipulating that I would double it! I did that, and it worked."

Porter, who has been teaching at the prestigious Milton Academy for the last two years, where she was faculty advisor for Stephen King's son, says that since "the publisher's office is right down at Park Street, in Boston, I've been able to pop in for an hour and sit down with the editor. I think a lot of young writers don't get that any more. I hate to say it, but it's usually sink or swim. The company's idea of letting me take my time, of working with me and bringing the book along, and sending me back to write it over and write it over, and . . . then sending me back to write it over and write it over paid off. And I have really liked the process. It was painful at times, and when you're teaching three classes and trying to work through your life, and writing a book, it can be a bit difficult."

The novel, a collective portrait of a black community in Lackawanna, near the steel mills of Buffalo, takes place during the hopeful and tragic 1960s. As Terry McMillan has written, the book is "an honest portrayal of folks who learned that the dream of economic freedom wasn't waiting for them 'up north,' " since they were the heirs to a dying industry. And in Porter's novel, the black families in the shabby company housing project of All-Bright Court are additionally circumscribed by their distrust and fear of all white people, although the few white people in this book are not the racist figures who have typically blocked the progress of black people.

"I think," said Porter, "that [the tension here] is more like a wariness, since very often in this book, blacks and whites don't even interract. This community, which is based on the actual one where I grew up, is very small and very insular. And 90 percent of the people in my neighborhood were transplanted southerners. So the parents often came up North with these specific ideas about how to raise children, and about how black children should interract with white children, and about how black children should go out into the world. And they brought those ideas from Alabama and Mississippi and Georgia, and transplanted them in this northern neighborhood."

Even in "today's ghettoes," she remarked, "there really isn't any interraction between blacks and whites, so the ideas never change. I remember that when I went away to college [at SUNY-Albany] and had a white roommate, I was the first black person she'd ever met in her life other than the person at the grocery store who puts your groceries in the bag. And that was pretty much the same experience that I had in Lackawanna. There were some whites in the neighborhood, and you saw them and you played with them and that was it; you get a bit of that in the book. When the school day was over, you went to your house, and they went to their houses, and when the work day was over, you went this way, and the other parents went that way, and you get that with the parents in the book too.

"There's another thing that happens with transplanted black southerners. In the South, racism was blatant. You knew what was what, and where not to go, and what not to do. I think that when blacks came North, without those walls there anymore, they had to take on this kind of encoded behavior of how to act and what to do, because there were no signs. There were no signs when the kids went to the pool that said they did not want black kids there, but no black people went there. You're not going to see any signs that say this kid should not go to this dance or you should not go in that bar, but parents begin to realize that this goes on and then they pass [their wariness] on to the kids—often with little or no explanation."

In *All-Bright Court* it is the novel's hero, Mikey, a gifted young man who is eventually sent to a private preparatory school in the Northeast, who confronts his mother on this issue. "The mother says something to him about 'white people,' and he says, 'How do you know? You don't know any *white people*.' And she screams, 'Shut up. What are you talking about?' The thing is, when I think about these characters, I realize that people don't know one another, and yet they have this very certain set of beliefs about what this other group does or what that other group is. A lot of those relationships happen because of fear. The [black] parents don't even want to run the risk" associated with change.

"Maybe it's just my own experience, but I think that so much fear separates people in this country along racial lines. If there is any hope out there, it is with younger people. There are so many people who, without any first-hand experience, are taught to distrust people, even to hate them, or at the least not to get close to them. Lorene Barry, who wrote *Black Ice* (about her experience as a black student in a largely white prep school during the early 1970s), had the same kind of message from her parents. Her father told her the story about this little girl who was told to jump down the stairs and the girl said, 'I can't.' Her father said, 'I'll catch you; I'll catch you.' So the kid jumps off, and he jumps out of the way, and then he says, 'Never trust anybody.' People don't get beyond the 'I can't trust anybody' or 'These people are my enemy.' Even in a place like Milton Academy, it seems like up to about the age of twelve or thirteen, everybody's okay. I don't know what happens to the socialization in this country, but after a certain age that's it."

Porter's hero, Mikey, faces the dilemma of how to remain part of his community while leaving it for the larger world. "He will have to figure it out," explained Porter "and his choice is not necessarily the best choice. I was talking to someone recently about this idea of the individual versus the community. Black people in this country have generally been community minded, and this person was asking if black people in this country should be more individual minded? I think the way to go lies somewhere in the middle. You have to be an individual within your community, but this idea that you should never have white people for friends" is, at the least, outdated. "The world used to be so different, even thirty years ago. Perhaps you did grow up in a community, and you stayed there your entire life; you never had to come into contact with white people except to go to work for them. But now, that's not reality. You have to get out there, and you have to get a job. You have to be able to live wherever it is you are going to live and work on whatever job you're going to work on. Sometimes you're on jobs where they say, 'You will be at that party on Friday night at nine o'clock.' In the past, blacks haven't had to deal with situations where you are almost forced to get out there and integrate. And if you go out there with the idea, *I can never trust these people, they are always going to do me in in the end,*' that can make for an almost schizophrenic person."

In Mikey's case, he "has to reconcile what it is that his parents are teaching him, which is to be wary," with their other message, which is "to go in that world but not to be of it at all." As his mother says, *"I'm not sending you to this school to make friends. I'm sending you to learn. Your friends right here in this house, hear me?"* Even though Mikey's parents acknowledge the private-school opportunities, they feel betrayed both by his departure and by how he changes. They understand that "once he's gone off he's left their world"—sentiments shared by all first-generation children and their parents. But in order to spare his parents these feelings of betrayal, Mikey would have to stay in All-Bright Court or a similar ghetto.

"These families were really migrants, almost immigrants to another country," said Porter. "They came from the South, from that Jim Crow world, and many of them, at least in my parents' generation, left an entirely different world to come to the North in the 1940s. I don't have to tell you what Birmingham, Alabama, was like in 1942. They came to a totally different world and, as with many immigrant experiences, the children learn another language that the parents are not speaking." Porter makes this point clear through the evolution of the narrator's speech in the book and by his parents' reaction to it: *"You done turned white, and you can't stay here. You got to go live with white folks,"* Mikey's father told him.

"The children take on a new language, take on new friends, take on an educational system that the parents never had any chance of getting into, and in a way the children do become these strangers that the parents have to figure out what to do with. It's an irony, too, that the parents must feel, 'Am I being left behind because my child is going on?' and that they have to live with it because this is really what they came to that country for: a better chance for the kids. The kids take that chance, and the parents are like, '*Oh, no!,*' but I think with Mikey he can hold on to more of what he's being told by his parents. . . . Sometimes I have ambivalent feelings about education. I think what's happening with Mikey is that he basically throws all the home stuff out."

The problem is illustrated during a crucial scene in *All-Bright Court* when Mikey repeats to a prep school friend a story about monkeys that his father told him when he was six and they visited the zoo. " *'I'm telling you,'* his father insisted, *'don't pay no attention to they screaming. They smart, smart enough to talk. But they won't, 'cause if they do, they know white people going to make them work. . . . It's true. My Daddy told me so.'"* Porter recalled "that stuff about monkeys talking," and pointed out that Mikey "doesn't take these stories as metaphorical. He takes them very literally as, 'Oh boy, these people are *crazy,*' and he doesn't see anything else."

Mikey's response reminded her of the time she "was writing a short story in graduate school, and it was written in dialect, but when the narrator was speaking, as opposed to writing, the story was in standard English although there were metaphors in there that people in the neighborhood would use. (The narrator was really someone like me who could sort of go back and forth.) I was so angry when this guy from California (who surfed and rode motorcycles) was telling me that poor people don't use metaphors and similes. I got so angry because I think poor people actually use metaphors and similes more than people who have an education, because they don't know exactly what it is they want to say. They will say, 'Somebody's hair looks like a row of corn' because *that's what it looks like,* and that's their point of reference.

"What happens with this boy, Mikey, is that he almost takes on an attitude that language, and the use of metaphor, and the use of simile, is for the classroom and is coming out of books, and what he is being taught by his parents can't somehow fall into that camp. What aggravates me about him is that he wants to throw all that folk knowledge away and keep solely what's in the books. More than anything else, that's what gets him into trouble. He wants to just take this one path and not consider that he can pick and choose what he needs."

Porter, who is a "Public Broadcasting System addict," said she was recently watching "The Frugal Gourmet" and "Jeff Smith was talking about the idea of food and what it does for people. It's interesting that the first generation gives up traditional food; in the later generations, when you become nostalgic, you realize that you almost needed to make that break—in order to get back to where you were." But Connie Porter hopes that "everybody doesn't have to have that experience. I've worked with kids who are from China or wherever, who are going through the same thing—'What do I take, and what do I give up, and how do I put it all in order when I look at this book and [the schools] tell me something totally different from what I'm learning at home?' And I really would hope that everyone who goes through this doesn't have to give up their whole history and their whole culture in order to drive a BMW and live in a townhouse. I think you can do both: 'Put on your James Brown records right in your townhouse!' Have your neighbors knocking, 'Turn that thing down!'

"I think that there can be a balance, but it's something that has to be worked at, because you rarely achieve balance at eighteen. What's sad, though, is when people at thirty or forty haven't worked it out at all and are still running away, whether they be black, Jewish, Chinese, Japanese, or Hispanic. They are running away, [and here Porter, who could have been a professional mimic, takes on a multiplicity of accents]: 'I don't want to deal with those people; I don't eat beans; I don't even like rice; I don't eat watermelon; I don't eat matzoh.' You do meet these people who have totally denied everything that they are. And in a way it's sad, because in a sense they become nothing. What they say is, 'I'm just a person; people are people.' True: But there's nothing wrong with being something specific."

On the other hand, Porter is wary of identification principally by racial or ethnic grouping, as currently practiced in the United States, and she worries about its implication for a unified society. "When I'm watching the TV news I really hate this sense of gloating about all this stuff that goes on in the Soviet Union. . . . 'Oh, they're breaking up, ha ha,' Look at this country in fifty years! It's easy to look at other places and say they're factionalized, but I would hope that in this great experiment called the United States there is some way to hold on to your own culture and to still come together as a country. I don't know whether we have struck that balance, or whether in fifty years Florida will say, 'We're leaving now! We're Cuban and Haitian, and we're going to be a Caribbean peninsula.' "

It's clear why Porter thinks she's "carrying a satire gene," although she has to tell her students that satire and humor are not the same thing. "Satire is my first love—Kurt Vonnegut and Jonathan Swift—and *Candide* is probably my favorite book of all time. I'd put that at the top of the list. I've read it a dozen times." Satire, she believes, "allows you to take a closer look at a society without the reader having his guard up . . . because you don't want to be on a soapbox and start preaching to people about race or issues of the environment. But if you take on a tone where people are laughing along with you, you can teach them something without them really knowing it, at least until the end! That's what I like the most about satire, that you can take on social issues in that way."

Another of Porter's favorite books is *The Jungle* by Upton Sinclair. "It gets to be too didactic at some point, but I like the section about the meatpacking, and the sausage, and people falling in the vats . . . until he got to the point where he was on a soapbox. It happened with Richard Wright, when he gets up on that soapbox. In the communism section [of *Native Son*], I wanted to scream, 'I got it, got it, got it, got it, got it!' And when she calls on satire in her own writing, Porter tries to "keep the message as short as possible."

Porter's life experience and her philosophical view inspired the "really dark satire" involving the murder of a young woman in a Buffalo housing project—not All-Bright Court—in the book she is writing now. "It reflects the changes that have happened in society in the last thirty years with this 'wilding' stuff. There was an incident in Boston where they killed a woman on Halloween, stabbed her about 130 times, and disemboweled her." When "they were interviewing these boys, what they came up with is that *they were bored, they didn't really have anything else to do, so they thought they'd go out and get somebody.* I began to think, 'Hey, what in the world has happened to kids, and I'm not just talking about black kids. That kind of behavior is indicative of something else that's going on, although I'm sure every generation asks this same question." Porter believes that "kids have not changed that much in the last several decades," but she wonders: "Where is this kind of violence coming from in the society? I don't think it is just television, or Rambo and Arnold Schwarzenegger. . . . It's also this displaced anger that kids have in this nuclear age, the idea that *'Come on now, we could all be dead in an hour.'* I'm trying to figure it out in writing this book.

"My estimation is that you have one kid or two kids who decide to do something, and then the next thing you know, they are with their friends and there are ten people there. Two kids do something, and ten people are charged, and then it's a big muddle. One thing that really aggravates me is this whole cottage industry that has risen up around these kinds of crime. There's the prosecutor, and the community activist, and the lawyers, and before you know it, there's a zoo. And its so difficult to get back to what happened to that one person. On the news last Sunday they were talking about civil rights with this group and that group and the chief of police. I'm sick of it. I mean, *can we get back to what happened?*

"In a way, people don't really want to examine what's going on. It's easier to get this whole zoo going. Call the kids *a bunch of animals,* and then ride the wave until somebody else gets killed, and then you get on that wave, and you keep on going."

This anger feeds Porter's desire to "write more about the larger picture and about individuals and how they interract, even if the society we're living in is [in the case of *All-Bright Court* and the forthcoming novel] a small community with a few hundred people. . . . It would be sad to pick up a novel fifty years from now that was written now and wonder what was going on." The same is true of television programs about black families. "My brother really cracked me up when he talked about this show, 'Fresh Prince of Bel Air' [a lighthearted look at the adventures of a black ghetto youngster who goes to live with his rich family in California.] I know the point that my brother is making, too. As he said, 'My God, black men are becoming extinct and this is the damn stuff they are showing on television?' How can you possibly have so many things going on and pick up a novel or see a television show that somehow does not address these problems? It's horrible to have this [sociological] famine and all we are seeing are shows about people feasting."

Porter points to John Edgar Wideman's novel, *Philadelphia Fire*, as "a book that gets to it. That story [about what happens when orders to bomb a black neighborhood were issued by the black mayor of Philadelphia] should have been written: *'Excuse me, this is the only time in America that a bomb was actually dropped by the government on somebody's house, trying to run these people out of there.'* And I'm glad that story found a market."

When Connie Porter was questioned by a friend about her recent success, she remembered that when she lived in Lackawanna, she "used to go to Woolworths and that used to be the biggest thing—to take the bus, because we lived in the boondocks, and you had to walk a half mile to *get* to the bus! I'd take the bus downtown with my mother, and the big thing was to sit at the counter and get an orange drink and a tuna sandwich on toast. I thought I was living large!" As she pointed out, "you always have that inner child in you. When I was at the Ritz with the publisher a few months ago, I did think, *'Oh my God, I'm in the Ritz tearoom.'* I mean, sometimes I do have experiences where I'm overwhelmed. The person who was so happy to sit at the Woolworths counter is now sitting at the Ritz, listening to the harp, and wondering what tea to order. . . . *Am I awake?*"

The answer is: Completely, and with your very perceptive eyes wide open.

BOOKS BY CONNIE PORTER

NOVELS

All-Bright Court. New York: Houghton Mifflin, 1991.

Fay Weldon

WHEN the British writer Fay Weldon reaches New York at the end of an exhausting tour to promote her novel, *The Cloning of Joanna May,* you won't find her in one of the glass towers that dot the city. Instead, Weldon, overloaded with well-stuffed shopping bags from the city's fanciest boutiques, charges through the lobby of her elegant, Old World Madison Avenue hotel on the way to a flower-bedecked suite. There, wearing new purple glasses "from L.A.," the thoroughly modern

Weldon is prepared to talk and laugh about masculine control, female comeuppance, genetic engineering, the meaning of names, and the differences between American and British novels.

Fay Weldon is best known in this country for *The Hearts and Lives of Men* (written originally as forty-eight episodes for the British weekly *Woman,* a magazine "with royalty in the middle pages and cookery all around") and for *Puffball* and *The Fat Woman's Joke*. She is identified especially with *The Life and Loves of a She-Devil,* which was unfortunately metamorphosed into a muddled mess of an American movie, starring Roseanne Barr and Meryl Streep, that crashed at the box office.

The novel is about Ruth ("a short, dismissive, sorrowful name") who is the hulking, fat, and wronged wife of Bobbo. Ruth, who ends up powerful and rich ("$2,563,072.45 on deposit in a Swiss bank"), uses that money to recreate herself, through a variety of plastic surgeries, as the svelte and glamorous writer, Mary Fisher, the "she-devil" who has stolen her husband. In fact, Ruth has her long legs removed, shortened, and replaced so that she will be the petite creature, "who has size four feet and last year spent $1,200.50 on shoes," that her husband favors. In the Susan Seidelman movie, unfortunately, Ruth's reincarnation happens only through a more sophisticated and professional makeup job, which misses Weldon's point: Women struggle against sexism but often conform to it.

Like all of Weldon's fiction, *The Life and Loves of a She-Devil* is both horrifying and funny, but underneath the satirical and ironic voice, Weldon has created a parable about evil and the many ways in which the oppressed, in this case women, often become their own victims. She laughingly admits that "I certainly see my novels as morality tales although I don't go round saying that on 'The Today Show' particularly. You don't sit there saying, 'They are morality tales' and watch the eyebrows go up. On the contrary, when they say, 'Do men read you?,' you say, swiftly, '*Younger* men find no problem.' That way, the older ones think they better read it too." After all, "One is not naive in all this, . . . but I certainly do see my novels as morality tales or parables which you then work over in your mind and come to your own conclusions about."

Weldon says that she doesn't provide "the answer. I don't say, 'Ruth is crazy. Fancy doing all that for a man?' But I do believe that Ruth was trying to become the other woman in a kind of peculiar, extended sisterhood. I mean, she was dealing with envy by becoming the envied object. She put all her good into the other woman and took all her bad."

Needless to say, without this explanation, many of Weldon's feminist readers were unenthusiastic about Ruth's solution to her wandering husband problem, and Weldon admits that sometimes she does not feel that she is "the heroine of the women's movement" and is, in fact, "considered by many as the great betrayer." She absorbs a lot of disapproval for her sometimes feminist, sometimes satirically antifeminist views, even though she repeatedly points out that "two-thirds of the world's work is done by women although one-half of the world refuses to acknowledge it. And only one-tenth of the world's property is owned by women, so they are, on the whole, slaves."

We talked about her eponymous heroine in *The Cloning of Joanna May,* a sixty-year-old childless Englishwoman (named Joanna May) who finds out suddenly that she has four clones— now thirty years old—who were created while she was under anesthesia for a phantom pregnancy. This experiment was formulated by her domineering and superrational ex-husband, Carl May, who spent most of his childhood chained to his parents' dog kennel—where he learned to bay at the moon—and is now, in true Weldon style, the captain of Britain's nuclear energy industry. ("Karl May," [1842–1912, once the most popular author of boys' books in Germany] turns out to be Hitler's favorite writer, but I didn't know that at the time.") At May's direction, and with the help of the local mad scientist, one of Joanna May's eggs was extracted, "irritated" into fertilization (no sperm necessary), and reproduced.

Beyond writing a good story, Weldon is aiming here at the continuing controversy over nature versus nurture, and she "is making a case for both." We talked about the well-publicized opinion among many American geneticists that behavior patterns, responses, aptitudes, something often referred to as "niceness," and even criminal tendencies are all determined by genes and by markers on your DNA. Weldon agrees that "it may be true," although "I don't think that societies can afford to let it be true, because it means they just abandon all notions of progress and because it is a very dangerous doctrine." She points out that "for Carl May the genetic marker for niceness must have been erased, so he grows up to be rational and he behaves rationally, although he's a bit neurotic when it comes to dogs. His only experience is one of being at the mercy of irrationality, and he becomes a rational man: What he has to say about nuclear energy is perfectly rational, and these fascist stances that he takes are actually the stances of reason, but reason without pity." He is obviously a product of disastrous nurturing.

As an example of "nature," Weldon suggested that "the aesthetic sensibility is genetic although not inevitable." She says that "you look at your children, and you do see them inheriting the taste for very specific things" and also inheriting "the way you look at things and objects. But it is in some of the children and not in others, and that you can see. Perhaps even a moral aesthetic is genetic," but the genetic imperative is influenced, says Weldon, "by the other things: the intervention of intelligence, of self-control, of thought, and of any amount of socialization and training." On the other hand, she said with a smile, "anybody who's ever had children can observe that some children are as much possessed by vileness as their parents. It is original sin which is born into them!"

Fay Weldon was serious for a moment when she said, "It's a very dangerous doctrine that suggests we are out of control of our own lives or out of the control of our own societies. We're not." She doesn't think destiny has that much to do with genetics; in *The Cloning of Joanna May,* Joanna's clones—now called Gina, Jane, Julie, and Alice—were implanted into the wombs of four very different mothers, and they have clearly emerged as four very different, grown-up women. They have in common Joanna's genes and a laundry list of problems with men. In a not too subtle way, Weldon provides each of her characters with a contemporary choice for women: Jane is an unhappy but ambitious executive; Julie is an unhappy and bored housewife; Alice is an unhappy, self-absorbed model; and Gina is a very unhappy, battered mother of four.

Weldon explained that their names are important because writers "name characters in the way that parents name children. Names reveal their parents' expectations for them, and the child will, to some extent, work that expectation out. 'Alice'," she feels, "is a female, pretty name that the parents of boys would choose for the only girl, who comes along later [in life]. You'd call that child 'Alice.' 'Jane' is an intellectual from parents who don't want her to be fancy or live by the mind. . . . 'Joans' are often practical and self-effacing or else work terribly hard not to be, since their parents placed the doom of 'Joan,' the ordinary name, upon them. 'Julie' is a female name for a daughter who attends to its business and combs its hair properly. 'Gina' is a sort of shortened name, as if she never had a longer one, and her mother couldn't even be bothered to give her a full name or to put up with Gina. 'Joanna' is, in a way, a child you mean to neglect. You mean it somehow to grow up on its own." Weldon wondered aloud: "If I called my child 'Joanna,' what would I be willing upon her? Something not fancy, something right down the middle, which is what she had to be." This particular Joanna is beautiful, but Weldon says that her parents didn't know that. They named her to be ordinary "even though her husband complains later that she was 'middle of middle.' Her parents weren't themselves particularly beautiful, but she happens to be beautiful, which happens to interfere and intervenes with her fate."

Since I had recently edited a collection of essays about characters named 'Anne' or 'Anna,' I was particularly interested in Weldon's views on the intrinsic meaning of those names: " 'Anna,' " she said, "is a fairly neutral name which, because of *Anna Karenina,* can be a romantic name, but 'Anne' would be out there washing up. 'Anna' has a romantic potential which she can or cannot fulfill." Weldon said that she too often thinks about names, in and out of fiction: "I went to Israel with a group of writers, four women, and I thought, 'How strange. We all have names that are not proper names, they don't fit down the middle, and they are names which none of us would have wanted.' There was Beryl, Iris, Faith, and Bernice."

Perhaps it is Joanna's name that prevents her from being emotionally traumatized by the cruel experiment devised by Carl May; and even though May has both of her lovers—an Egyptologist and her gardener (shades of Lady Chatterly)—murdered, the reader gets to watch as Joanna bonds with her "sisters / twins, clones, children," and as they collectively triumph. (May, on the other hand, dies in a Chernobyl-like explosion that is triggered by his own insufferable ego.)

Nor is Bethany, May's red-haired mistress and the author's favorite character in this novel, devastated by the machinations of Carl May. Since this is a Fay Weldon novel, this particular mistress wears "high crocodile shoes, ginger stockings, and chains of gold butterflies round neck, waist, and ankle," reads books about nuclear energy, and goes to the theater. Weldon gleefully recounted that Bethany is "an unusual name for bimbos, and Joanna complains about it. But Bethany does her duty as 'bimbo' ["the look of the wanton was intentional and as fake as her orgasms"] and does what she can in a naughty way because she knows what her role is and follows it through. If you're going to be a bimbo, you'd better be a good one. She's very bright; she has an intellect." And, Weldon added, with a hearty and very mischievous laugh, Bethany understands "that it's one thing to appear ignorant and quite another to be ignorant. And she's not. She manages to live her life and be that person quite charitably although she's both been pushed into and conceded to live this life. And, in a way, why should she not?"

In fact, when Weldon explains that she herself was "brought up not to complain, that's my training, which probably shows," you can understand her affection for Bethany. "There is no point in being sorry for yourself," she believes, "because nothing happens. If you cry when you are a child and there's a parent around, the parent will do something about it. When you're an adult there is no parent, so you look after yourself." In other words, Fay Weldon will give her fictional women permission for all kinds of riotous or ruinous behavior, but not one ounce of tea or sympathy for incompetence, complicity with chauvinists, or passivity about sexism. Since her own parents were divorced when she was five years old, she was raised in an all-female household—mother, sister, grandmother—and was "brought up believing the world was female, whereas men have always believed the world is male. It's unusual for women to suffer from my delusion."

Perhaps part of the confusion about Weldon's rare brand of feminism stems from her current belief that "men are just as much victims of human nature as women are, although women are merely more obviously so." She thinks humane behavior has very little to do with gender. "I think it has to do with power. If you put a woman in a man's position, she will be more efficient, but no more kind," since it is "people who are wicked."

Nor does Weldon believe in actions without consequences. She skewered that idea in *The Hearts and Lives of Men* when she described a passionate sixties relationship: Clifford, the art dealer, and his girlfriend Helen, she said, want it all—"Sex without babies, revolution without poverty, careers without selfishness, art without effort . . .—Dinner, in other words, and no washing up."

At the other end of the spectrum from the "dinner . . . and no washing up" group, Weldon also has words for those repressed and depressed women who emerge so often in American novels, if only to retreat to their beds. "It occurs to you one day that it is not enough to pose a problem. It used to be that a lot of people, and especially Americans, thought that by defining a problem you could solve it, that there was some kind of in-built solution. A lot of women's writing continues to define the problem without actually saying that it is not enough to go into a room and put the covers over your head. . . . I mean, it's just boring. Bring that woman out and let her enjoy her misery!" Although she agrees that Joanna May also gets depressed, she does not climb into bed and stay there. "The bed is the trap. She's more sensible, and she doesn't get into the trap." Perhaps, I suggested, that ability to remain untrapped is much more British than American. But Weldon says, "In the first novel I wrote, *The Fat Woman's Joke,* that's what [the female character] does: She leaves her home, and she goes to a basement area with barred windows. She goes down there, and she won't go upstairs, and she eats and eats all the time. And when her nice little friend on her tottery heels comes down the steps and says, 'What are you doing to yourself?' she explains to her what the world is like out there and its general injustice, and she refuses to be part of it. Finally her husband arrives and says, 'You have to come out of there.' " So, "I think I got rid of it in that novel, and I never had to do it again. . . . I wonder if this is a male vision of women that women pick up?"

Weldon says that this plot would not be "any more true in real life then that Darcy would marry Elizabeth, but we have to believe it anyhow! Let's see, Mrs. Bennett retires to bed for her nerves, doesn't she? And women in men's fiction sort of go to their rooms (or they're sent to their rooms), and where else is there to go?" To prove that nothing has changed, she mentioned "a lovely, coming-of-age book by an English writer," in which a father leaves, and "the mother, having taken to religion, goes to stay with her sister, goes to bed, and gets terribly fat. And then she comes out of her room and the sign of her improvement or her recovery from depression, is to go on a diet, get slim, and meet another man."

Weldon thinks that the only space women have if they want the approval of men, and editors, and publishers, "is the conventional inward-turning into their sensitivities and their sensibilities, by which somehow they are meant—in their usual nurturing fashion—to look inward and produce. I think it is just conventional behavior and conventional writing for women. And I don't do it." Some writers who are women "want approval, and

I just never needed approval. I like approval like anybody else, but I don't need it and I don't depend on it."

When you look at women's lives, Weldon said, "you end up with the feeling that there is no solution, and you have to look at the facts of the matter. . . . If the world has been run and ruled by men for many years because they find women inadequate, well perhaps the women are." She continued with typical British tongue-in-cheek: "I think you have to consider it. If things are universally held, they are not necessarily so, but they may be so. After all, it was once universally held that the earth was flat, so they may not be so. On the other hand, I think you owe [this idea] the courtesy of consideration. You can't just instantly say, 'Oh, all those things are wrong.' I'm not saying it's so after all those centuries, but it may be that women are not just conditioned into passivity, not just conditioned into loving children.

"Look what happened in Ireland. . . . The marriage rate in Europe was one in three until this century, and for the first part of the century only one woman in three in Ireland was married because the penalty of marriage was children and the penalty of children was death—because you died and your children died. We all know that children died, but it was more than that. After your sixth baby, *you* usually died. So now we have sort of gone into a world in which we expect the satisfaction of our desires. We used to think that going out to work was wonderful, and that staying at home was terrible and doing nothing, and indeed you died of boredom and pointlessness, and when you went out to work, at least you got to see your friends and play the power games that men play and that women enjoy playing as well."

How do you resolve it? I asked. "You decondition women, you make society around them so pleasant that they, in fact, have a choice in the way they live their lives."

When Weldon visited the Soviet Union a few years ago she decided that nothing positive had occurred where women were concerned. "It was rather horrifying to discover that one of the first things they were doing with *perestroika* was to have a Miss

Russia contest! All they were saying is, really, 'We're so bored with our women looking so awful, we're prepared to bring back capitalism so that we don't have to look at them anymore.'

Weldon, who has four children, has been married to the jazz musician / painter Ron Weldon for more than twenty-five years. Her four sons, three of them with Weldon, were born over a period of twenty-one years, at seven-year intervals, so that she would not have more than one small child underfoot. "An older child packs its own bag and ties its own shoes. And you can function as a human being, as a human woman, with one child. The minute you have two children, there is no way you are not a mother. You then leave the human race." Having four children, and the last one at age forty-six, has made Weldon see childbirth as "one of the areas of greatest social change, . . . the difference in style from one to the next, the idea of what a baby is and how you behave—anesthesia and no anesthesia; father present and no father present; all the breastfeeding and all the no breastfeeding; all the stitching up and all the no stitching up; all the shaving and all the not-shaving. And [with each child] always something had changed. . . . "

Fay Weldon spends part of the week in London in an office with computers, office help, laser printers, and fax machines and the rest of the time in a country farmhouse where there are sheep, ducks, and geese. She often writes her novels on the trains that carry her back and forth. In addition, Fay Weldon spends a good bit of time in the United States every year when each new novel appears, and she is a prolific reader of both American and British novels. Before the interview ended, I pressed her to express those differences she perceived between American and British fiction. "I think," she said, "there is a national difference that has to do with the fact that American writers [who are women] feel their woes to be legitimate and we don't. . . . And this has to do with the concept of the self, the I that sort of narrates a life, and the you that is seen by other people. The distress in one's life comes from the fact that the I and the you don't somehow coincide. They overlap, but they don't coincide: the eyes you look out of and the self that looks different. In American women, that I that is looking out is much more powerful. English women tend to live in the periphery of their lives," and while that "tends to make them good observers, they don't feel entitled to their griefs or their woes. They're not allowed to go back to bed and put the covers over their heads. You have to do the washing up and go out because there is no sympathatic observer out there, and the I is not strong enough to legitimize the feelings. It's easier for Americans. Their sense of entitlement and outrage is greater, even though, oddly, in the novels they retreat to bed."

"But," said Weldon, with a laugh, "I don't." Good, I thought, because then Fay Weldon's many devoted readers would have been denied these characters and stories, and all the Russian, British, and American women-haters, men-bashers, victims, and social deviants who are no doubt on the way.

BOOKS BY FAY WELDON

NOVELS

The Fat Woman's Joke—McKay, 1968; Chicago: Academy Chicago Publishers, 1986.

Down Among the Women. New York: St. Martin's, 1972; Chicago: Academy Chicago Publishers, 1984.

Female Friends: A Novel. New York: St. Martin's, 1974; Chicago: Academy Chicago Publishers, 1988.

Remember Me. New York: Random House, 1976; Ballantine, 1985.

Words of Advice. New York: Random House, 1977.

Little Sisters. unavailable.

Praxis. New York: Summit, 1978; Penguin, 1990.

Puffball. New York: Summit, 1980; Penguin, 1990.

The President's Child. New York: Doubleday, 1983.

The Life and Loves of a She-Devil. New York: Pantheon, 1984; Ballantine, 1985.

The Shrapnel Academy. New York: Viking, 1987; Penguin, 1988.
The Hearts and Lives of Men. New York: Viking, 1988; Dell, 1989.
The Heart of the Country. New York: Viking, 1988; Penguin, 1988, 1990.
Leader of the Band. New York: Viking, 1989; Penguin, 1990.
The Cloning of Joanna May. New York: Viking, 1990; Penguin, 1991.
Darcy's Utopia. New York: Viking, 1991; Penguin, 1992.
Life Force: A Novel. New York: Viking, 1992.

SHORT STORIES

Watching Me, Watching You. New York: Summit, 1981.
The Rules of Life. (short novel) New York: Harper & Row, 1987.
Polaris & Other Stories. New York: Penguin, 1989.
The Wife's Revenge & Other Stories. London: Masterworks UK, 1990.
Moon Over Minneapolis. New York: Penguin, 1992.

NONFICTION

Letters to Alice: On First Reading Jane Austen. New York: Taplinger Publishing Co., 1985; Carroll & Graf, 1990.
Rebecca West. New York: Viking, 1985; Penguin, 1985.
Sacred Cow: A Portrait of Britain, Post-Rushdie, Pre-Utopia. London: Chatto & Windus, 1990.

PLAYS

Mixed Doubles, n.d.
Action Replay. London; New York: S. French, 1980.
I Love My Love. London; New York: S. French, 1984.
Woodworm, n.d.
Jane Eyre: An Adaptation, n.d.
The Hole in the Top of the World, n.d.

Joy Harjo

THE Ford Foundation building on the east side
of Manhattan is one of those steel and glass towers that most people associate with New York City.
But the thirteen-story space that would usually
serve as a lobby is in this case a hidden paradise,
within the glitter and grime of the city; it has running brooklets, bubbling fountains, mature flow-
ering dogwoods and cherry trees, and clusters of
asters and marigolds near every path. It was here
that I spoke with Joy Harjo—Native American

poet and writer, member of the Creek (Muscogee) tribe, then associate professor of English at the University of Arizona at Tucson, and tenor sax player—in a borrowed office, at the tag end of her East Coast speaking tour.

In 1990 Harjo won one of the first annual PEN Oakland–Josephine Miles Awards for Excellence in Literature (which promote a multicultural viewpoint) for *In Mad Love and War,* but she is also the author of *She Had Some Horses* (which has almost reached cult status among other writers and poets) and a chapbook called *Secrets from the Center of the World.* Adrienne Rich has called her "one of the real poets of our mixed, fermenting, end-of-century North American imagination," and this description of Harjo seems particularly apt. Although Harjo says that she "can't speak for all Indian women," that she can't represent all Indian women, since "even in my own tribe there are many differences," it seems clear that her Native American inheritance is the greatest influence on her poetry, her angle of vision, and on the resolute, determined, and very serious persona that the non–Native American interviewer sees: "I talk more and laugh more when I am with Indian people. We are a very humorous people, yet the image that people have of us is as stoic and quiet. But that perception comes from outsiders. Indian peoples who not many years ago were 100 percent of the human population of this continent are now one-half of 1 percent of the population. But I move as who I am through all of these spaces, and I have conflicts in both worlds."

It is particularly noticeable when you talk with Joy Harjo that this writer is involved with more than fame and money. Perhaps her focus also emanates from her ethnic and spiritual background, since she remains convinced that "many artists have separated themselves from the community, and in a sense art has been separated from the community and that has to do with commerce . . . and with big business." The ideal community "has its roots in tribal communities, which we all were," says Harjo, and that community "has become fractured. In the ideal community, the value of the visionaries—the musicians and writ-

ers—was in what they did [and still do] for the community, and
their contributions were seen as crucial to the community's health.
In an ideal society, artists would be respected and valued for
their work, and would be paid to do that work by the rest of the
society because of what they give back."

Unfortunately, as all poets and readers of poetry know, that
utopia has not materialized. Like many poets, Harjo must teach,
lecture, and perform in order to make a living. Fortunately for
her, she is "also doing screenwriting," which she sees as "writing
long poems and moveable poems, and that is a lot more lucrative."

Everything Harjo does, however, must be codified by her personal, internalized sense of ethics. Right now, for instance, she
believes that she's "supposed to be teaching and saying what I'm
saying. It's taken me a while to . . . enter into an academic institution, because I've always had internal conflicts regarding those
places. To be part of such institutions always sets up this conflict. But now I've come to a place where I see that I'm truly
useful, and I don't think I'm selling out at all." In fact, "I feel like
I'm finally accepting myself and thinking, 'I can go into that
place and teach a class in a way that defies convention, and I
can teach poetry and literature in a manner that is regenerative
and respectful of the community. But there's "always the danger
because you're there. (You have to watch out for the places you
go because you could 'take on' that institution . . . or that place.)
So I watch myself: Am I becoming what I don't want to be? And
yet, these institutions employ some people who have vision, who
have heart, and who truly love what they are doing and see the
connections between what they are doing and the people. And
then there are always the others, who appear to be the majority,
who are divorced from anything, even from themselves."

What energizes Harjo to stay in the classroom, at least for the
time being, is exemplified by a story she told me about a pivotal
teaching experience. One of her students "did a project for the
class. She went to a couple of nursery schools and asked the
children, who were two to two and a half years old, to draw a

picture of an Indian and every one of them drew either a blood-thirsty savage, a generic Plains Indian with a tomahawk, or idealized Indian princesses. False images were already encoded."

This kind of experience is compounded by what Harjo calls the problem of the "John Wayne psyche in America. I attended this Five Years of Resistance Conference in Ecuador with native peoples from all over. A native woman from Bolivia said, 'We thought that John Wayne had killed everybody off. We were so touched to see you people [meaning North American native peoples] come down here because we thought that you were dead, that there was no one left.'

"In the American conscience, there are no Indians anymore because we don't dress the way we used to, we don't live the way we used to. Certainly, with humans, change is the primary force. If you're not growing and moving, you're dead." But non–Native Americans "want to keep us frozen in the moment before any guilt was able to happen, because it feels safer to keep us frozen in that space. I think many native writers destroy that space. It's a destructive space.

"For America to really change, it must become a society that regenerates the earth. Otherwise we will not last because the dynamic system of the planet has no use for you. . . . It's important as a writer to do my art well and do it in a way that is powerful and beautiful and meaningful, so that my work regenerates the people, certainly Indian people, and the earth and the sun. And in that way we all continue forever." At some point "there is no separation, and we all come from the same place."

Harjo believes that "it's important for work to be regenerative, to go back and to address the past because as long as there is that respect and acknowledgment of . . . connections, then things continue working. But when that stops, we all die. When what we do does not generate the earth, then there is no need for us anymore. . . . If you think of the way human beings are, especially in this country and other so-called highly civilized, well-developed countries, how does the earth benefit from our presence?"

Harjo's presence in the classroom proves useful in another way as well. Like most people on American campuses today, she is all too aware of the continuing, sometimes fruitless arguments about "opening the canon," an endless, usually internecine battle over the inclusion of women, minorities, and culturally diverse voices in the literary and history curricula. "Most institutions in the 1990s," she believes, "are giving voice to that [debate] because they are being forced to. But I would say that many of them aren't sincere about it. Certainly it's something that is being talked about, but the implementation of [canon revision] comes down to certain professors. You can't get Professor So-and-So, who hates women and who doesn't feel that literatures based in oral traditions have any literary value, to change. You can't force people." Reading lists that do not include these voices, she thinks, are "still . . . the norm."

Even Harjo's own students are often part of the problem. "I get people who usually know that I am an American Indian and a poet, so I think they expect something a little different. But you still get people who are almost shocked by another system and another way of thinking because their education from kindergarten is based on an exclusion of other ways of thinking and exclusion of women. Particularly in the case of American Indian cultures, . . . the education most of my students have is based on nonreality. It is based on television. . . . That's how they have primarily loaded their brain cells."

Harjo would like her students to understand that native and American myths "are highly present and highly charged events in our lives now, informing us in our own actions." If they understand that "the ancestors never left us, that they are present, and that the stories that they were (and are) involved in are played out now," they will comprehend "that everything we do touches on those [ancestral myths] and that the system is a regenerative system, and not static and closed. You evoke those ancestors when you tell the stories, and that way they stay alive, they stay with you, and they are part of you."

Part of the "problem in American society, because certainly I am an American and I think about these things, is the lack of myths that codify and unify a community. When I think of American myths (and I talk about this in my classroom), I think of Elvis Presley, Marilyn Monroe, John Wayne, Madonna. These are all myths that were created. What do these myths represent? The value system. They are all people who have been created in a commercial system.

"All people have spiritual needs (and I'm not talking about church), . . . but we all need spiritual food, which I think poetry is. . . . We all have that need, and myths fulfill it. The poets and musicians reinvigorate them, but, at the same time, myths do the same thing to us because they are alive and they are present."

Would the myths change if the poet moved from the space she was in to another place, I asked? "Some people," she said, "would say that. I talked to Navajo people who think that when you are within the four sacred mountains you are within the circle of myth, so to speak. [The four sacred mountains are Blanca Peak, Colorado (Sis Naaini), sacred mountain of the east; Mount Taylor, New Mexico (Tsoodzil), sacred mountain of the south; San Francisco Peaks, Arizona (Dook'o'oostiid), sacred mountain of the west; and the the La Plata Mountains, Colorado (Dibe' Nitsaa), sacred mountains of the north.] But when you leave those, you are more vulnerable, and more susceptible to danger and to loss. I think about my own tribe (I am not a fullblood, so there is already a mixing that goes on, but I am a tribal member). Since we were moved and *forcibly* moved from the southeastern United States because Andrew Jackson's relatives needed land— these things are always based on something very personal—there was a very painful tearing away from a place where the myths grew. Certainly I do think some of them follow you; you carry them, you evoke them when you tell the stories. In that way they stay alive, they stay with you, . . . they are part of you.

"Of course there are some things that can never be replaced. So you work and you struggle to create and build your life. Now I see that . . . I can be in Oklahoma or in New Mexico, and whatever is missing from my heart," the myths and stories "are always with me."

About six years ago, when Harjo was teaching at the University of Colorado at Denver, she began to study the saxophone, more or less on her own. She joined a big band there and although she was under the impression it was going to be for beginners, there were "professionals and semiprofessionals, and it was like learning to swim by being pushed off the high diving board. I just kept it up. Once in a while I'd get a lesson somewhere, but it's only been very recently that I've begun to study—not full time, since I feel that I am doing four things full time. I'm interested in jazz, r-and-b, and tribal music, and in combining traditions, and in finding another way to work with poetry that involves oral art. There are poets," she says "who write more for the page, but for me, poetry is based on . . . language, words, and how those things sound. (I've started a band—Poetic Justice.)"

We talked, too, of poetic images, of flight juxtaposed with stagnation, and of the illusory quality of imagination and memory. Those images resonate in her verse essay, "Northern Lights": "Bells, the occasional sacred flute like wind beneath an eagle, and the drum marking more than time, rather outlining ancestors, a pipeline into the earth to the mother of volcanoes. . . . What must have been the Head Crow laughed from a stiff telephone wire, swung back and forth beneath the sun, blinking his eyes at the sleeping pitiful world" (*The American Voice*, pp. 45–47).

Harjo says, "I think about how space moved when I was a child and I used to fly. I could fly out, and I went to the stars, and I would fly to the moon, and it wasn't something that I imagined. It really happened." When she is writing she has "the sensation of flying, of moving through space," and the element with which she feels most comfortable is "probably the air. . . . I realize that there are many air images of clouds, planets in my work." Apparently, many critics have pointed out that her "poems happen all over the place . . . in Ashland, Wisconsin, in Chicago." All of this "goes back to my tribe's forced movement. I joke and say, 'Well, I keep moving so they can't find me.' But that isn't the whole story."

The poetry of Joy Harjo, which she says is "a way to speak our language again, a sacred language, and to be in touch with the sacred places more consistently," is admired by many readers and listeners. When she read recently at the City Center in New York, her large and attentive audience contained both Native and non–Native Americans. But for Harjo her "first audience, the first circle or the inner circle, is of course my people. But," she adds, "I am an American citizen and a citizen of the world and of the universe. And I think my work addresses common concerns and common music in its own very particular ways."

BOOKS BY JOY HARJO

POETRY

The Last Song. Las Cruces, New Mex.: Puerto Del Sol, 1975.
    (A chapbook)
What Moon Drove Me to This? New York: I Read Books, 1979.
She Had Some Horses. New York: Thunder's Mouth Press, 1983.
Secrets from the Center of the World (photographs by Stephen Strom). Tucson: Sun Tracks, University of Arizona Press, 1989.
    (A chapbook)
In Mad Love and War. Middletown, Ct.: Wesleyan University Press, 1990.

Jane Smiley

YOU'VE heard the cliché about how "into every person's life some rain must fall." But when you make your living interviewing people, you gingerly try to avoid that inevitable day when the monsoons are swirling in from the east, the hurricanes are blowing up from the south, and in the north it's snowing. Suffice it to say, the interview with Jane Smiley took place that day.

Smiley, the author of *The Age of Grief* (a short-story collection nominated for the National Book

Critics' Circle Award), *The Greenlanders,* (588 pages), the much acclaimed set of novellas *Ordinary Love and Good Will,* and *A Thousand Acres* (loosely based on the King Lear story), which won the National Book Critics' Circle Award and the Pulitzer Prize in 1992, is a full professor of English at Iowa State University in Ames. But she was on a speaking tour of upstate New York when we agreed to meet in Kingston at the local Greyhound station. She would pick me up there in her rented car, and we would proceed to a coffee shop in the sixties hippie hangout of Woodstock, New York, where we would talk books over the ubiquitous croissants.

I left my house in New Jersey and proceeded to the Port Authority in New York City with what I thought was a reasonable amount of cash. Unfortunately, I had forgotten about the entrenched paranoia at the Greyhound counter where they now accept only cash for all bus tickets and where to a Visa card they "just say No." So much for most of that cash. I boarded a bus that was so packed that I was forced to sling my bookbag onto the rack above the seats. As luck would have it, our driver, Mr. Personality, jammed on the breaks as he rounded the first curve, and my tape recorder, supposedly at home in that same bookbag, flew out and across the aisle where it missed a fellow passenger's head by inches. Had it hit, I would have had not only a shattered tape recorder on my hands, but a hefty lawsuit. What I did have was not enough money, or time, to buy a new tape recorder.

I spent the next two hours on the bus convincing myself that Smiley would surely have a tape recorder (she did not), or that one of the local bookstores would certainly have a radio / cassette player (no to this one) or tape recorder, and that somebody in such a laid back arts colony would lend us one. (Answers: No, they didn't, and, in any case, No, they wouldn't.) After running around Woodstock for one hour (and since Jane Smiley is six feet, two inches tall, when you walk with her, you run!), we found ourselves sitting on the floor of the local framing gallery using the boombox of the owner, who had managed to melt together most of its buttons with her trusty blow torch. After this unfortunate preamble, the writer and I talked books, money, and publishing.

Jane Smiley is from St. Louis. While she gleefully disappoints an easterner's expectations about the good-natured souls in the center of the country she says, "Basically, I'm always satisfied. I'm from the Midwest, and people from the Midwest feel lucky to be invited, you know? We try to wipe our mouths after we eat, and keep our hands below the table, and speak when spoken to. But it's a good pattern too, in some ways, because for your own mental health you don't go around saying, 'I should have had this; I should have had that,'" all signs of excellent mental health in New York City. "In the Midwest, we say to ourselves, 'Gee, I got this; I got that' and 'Wow, they didn't have to give me anything.' And I guess there is a group of people in the country, whether they are Midwesterners or middle class, or whatever their background is, whose parents tell them all their lives: 'Just be happy you got anything.' And it's not bad."

The Midwestern message notwithstanding, Smiley has plenty to say about the marketing of novels and publicity tours. For instance, "I want to be sent on the road like any man and not be kept in tissue paper back at the office. Why aren't they sending the women writers out? Most readers in America are women, and not every male writer is a sex machine either. As far as promoting books [and publishing issues are] concerned, there is a kind of cronyism." (This problem was remedied when Smiley had a national tour for *A Thousand Acres,* even before it was one of five books nominated for the Book Critics Circle Awards in 1991.)

She recalled an incident at Alfred A. Knopf, her publishing house, where an author and his editor were "denouncing the review of the author's latest book. What they were truly incensed about was that the reviewer did not view the book as a 'Great American Novel'—and those letters were capitalized in their way of talking about it. I laughed. I was just standing outside the office and I laughed. . . . I would never in a million years even want to be writing the Great American Novel. I would never want to squash all the competition like that. *To me, the promise of fiction is the promise that everyone gets to speak, that every voice is heard,* and we listen to one, and we listen to the other, and we listen to the third, and that's the glory of being a reader and being a writer. And writing the Great American Novel is kind of like writing the last movie: Once this movie is finished, no movies will ever have to be made again. . . . All this just opened my eyes. It was actually quite funny."

She recounted an incident when she was driving with the writers Thomas Sanchez and Philip Caputo to Iowa City, where Sanchez and Smiley would give a joint reading of each other's work. On the way, the two men told stories about their careers and the careers of the men that they knew that made her realize there was a world she did not have access to. "After I thought about it, I realized that the men writers they were talking about were the hypermasculine ones like Tom McGuane and Thomas himself and Phil himself—ones who had had adventures. And then there were the editors. The editors brought money to the table, and the writers brought adventures—very masculine adventures—and the editors wanted to participate in the adventurous lives that the writers had had, and the writers wanted the money. And they were trading. They were trading something that's really quite abstruse for something that's really quite tangible. But the editors brought hundreds of thousands of dollars to the table because that was the only thing they had to impress these very male men with, and they would go down to Smith and Wollensky [a steak house in New York], and they would horsetrade. And sometimes—if they got on the bad side of one another—they'd shit on each other in a particularly male way."

The most obvious next question was, What do women who write get instead of that? "We get to be published," Smiley continued, "in a quiet way for a few thousand dollars, and we get some good reviews, and we get to avoid both the exaltation of lots of money and the humiliation of a big negative balance." The point is that "the men editors aren't out to impress us with big quantities of money because they don't want to buy our experiences! But I'm not going to say that publishing is worse or even as bad as any of the other male endeavors. On the scheme of things that includes commodities trading, making movies, big oil, big oil tankers, where's publishing here? I mean, publishers aren't even as mean as English professors in Ivy league universities."

Although Smiley does not rule out the possibility that men in publishing might have a positive influence on her career, she notes, "My editor is a woman, my agent's a woman, my Hollywood agent's a woman, and my best friend is a woman." I asked if women in publishing were, in effect, creating a club in order to better balance the equation. Smiley thinks they are. "My best friend is now the publisher of Scribner. She is a woman. My agent is probably more aggressive than any man, and she is intensely competitive, intensely straightforward, and she gets away with a certain amount of pure aggressiveness because she is a woman and they will listen to her. My editor, who is not aggressive, is a genius at reading and is extremely painstaking. And so what I might give up in power, I gain in terms of goodness, and I'm willing to make that bargain.

"I'm also willing to look back and say, 'Circumstances have been this, this, and this for each book.' For example, no one really expected The Age of Grief to do much, so they were caught short, and they didn't send me on the road. But things have changed at Knopf in the last couple of years. They are promoting more aggressively than they used to. They did put a lot of money behind The Greenlanders, and they did promote it in a lot of ways, but they hadn't made up their minds at that point to send people on the road to do the dog-and-pony show that other publishers were doing. They did print a lot of copies of The Greenlanders, and they did have high hopes for it, and it didn't pan out, as far as their hopes went.

"With The Greenlanders I really wanted to write the saddest book anybody ever read, but I didn't want it to be depressing. It sold exactly the way I thought it would. It had a narrow but deep appeal, and I knew it was going to be too obscure and too hard to be a bestseller. So I was a little nervous about such a large printing. I didn't think it was going to [be a bestseller], but it did pretty well.

"With *Ordinary Love and Good Will*, we tried to talk them into a large printing—35,000 or 40,000 copies—and they said, 'It's two novellas; nobody buys novellas; novellas are a drag on the market, blah, blah, blah.' They printed 10,000 copies. And my agent said, 'This is Jane Smiley's newest book; you have to promote this.' And then they were caught once again with their pants down, because they got great reviews and everything was sold, and they had seven [subsequent] printings, and they were always behind." And the bookstores, as often happens in publishing, could not obtain books. "Knopf said, 'Oh, we sold 18,000 copies, we're so glad.' My agent said, 'You could have sold 50,000; you should be pissed.' And I think, 'Well, they probably could have sold thirty if they'd been on the ball.'" In any case, "they did seven printings and now it's ready to be in paperback."

Whatever happens, Smiley, whose novellas *Ordinary Love and Good Will* received a front page review in the *New York Times Book Review,* is enjoying her success. Both stories, as Michiko Kakutani has written, "examine the closed circle of marriage and family that excludes others and that can sustain or suffocate those who live within its bounds." Rachel, Smiley's narrator in *Ordinary Love,* although the mother of five small children, manages to find time for an affair with a neighbor (a writer) who lives down the road. She tells her husband that she does not intend to stop seeing this man, and he responds by throwing her out of the house, taking the children out of summer camp (without her knowledge), selling the house, and moving to England, all within a few days. As they approach adulthood, one by one the children return, and the story opens as they are gathered for the return of one of the (male) twins from India. Smiley says that "Rachel has released herself from patriarchy, and therefore she is in the habit—and has been for twenty years—of considering her thoughts sincerely and truly. What she has not done, maybe out of natural reticence or out of habit, is to include her children in her self-knowledge. It's not that she hasn't communicated with them, but she's been reticent with them.

"I think that's common for women. I discovered that when I was divorced, and then single for two years, and then began having a relationship with the person who is now my husband and who then lived in California, that it was very easy for me to throw off motherhood, fly out to California, be wildly passionate, fly home, take on the mantle of motherhood, and go back in the house. When he came to live with me, one of the great resistances I had was being passionate in the same house where my children were, even if the doors were closed, even if they were asleep. The idea that sexual passion could be in the house with them was frightening to me. He noticed that I was very changed. It took us a few months for me to learn consciously to allow passion in the door.

"Then I thought back on my marriage to my previous husband, and I concluded that part of the purpose (but also part of the problem) of marriage itself is that once the children come, life is so daily and sort of routine. It encourages passion to go out the door, both for the father and the mother. That gives them the opportunity to avoid the discomfort of having passion in the family and what it provokes.

"To me this was very illuminating, and that's when I began to think about Rachel. Rachel, in her consideration of herself as a mother, just doesn't consider passion as part of herself even though it's been there from time to time. Her children don't consider passion as part of her, and when she reveals herself as a woman, the only one [of her adult children] who is willing to accept this idea of her is the one who himself has gone far enough down the destructive road of uncontrolled passion that he can recognize it, and hold his hand out to her, and say, 'I've been there too.' And the others don't want to, because their model of male / female relationships is a conjugal, family-oriented one."

The second novella, *Good Will,* concerns Bob Miller, a Vietnam veteran, for whom, as Josephine Humphreys said in the

Times, "the idea of living self-sufficiently becomes an obsession." He lives with his wife, Liz, and his young son, Tommy, on a farm in rural Pennsylvania on an annual income of $343.67, without a car, television, telephone, or any "real connection to the outside world except Tommy's daily trips to school. . . . Creepiness gradually invades the narrative, looming over Bob's self-created Eden. Something's going bad, very bad. Something's sneaking up on Bob, *and he doesn't see it coming.*" All of this becomes more understandable when Smiley says that she's "interested in isolated groups. (I always thought you could title all my books 'small group theory 1, 2, 3, 4.') . . . It seems to me that when a group is isolated or cut off (and this is also true of *The Greenlanders),* the dynamics are fairly pure. The idiosyncracies become more idiosyncratic, and the isolates begin speaking a new language. They mutate—like becoming a separate species—and develop weird characteristics, and they adapt very closely to the microenvironment that they live in. And when others invade from without, they look strange to the outsiders. They are clearly no longer in the mainstream and then they have a hard time, as their microenvironment changes, . . . adapt[ing] back to the mainstream."

About this particular isolate, Bob, who loses everything at the novella's end, Smiley thinks it's sad. "It's so clear that he was riding for a fall, and in your own mind you are saying, 'Watch out.' It's clear what's happening to him—he's at fault in some ways, his fall is deserved—but *the suspense lies in watching happen what you know is going to happen.* He set his life up in a way that I think was a mistake. He set himself up to be *isolated,* and he was trying to achieve a kind of purity. It was like *chutzpah,* but he didn't understand it as a matter of pride; he just understood it as a matter of desire. He had the talents, the opportunity, the time, and he could do it. So he made the fairly minor choice to try and live without money. But what he discovered, as his life worked itself out, was how overwhelmingly restrictive that choice was and how, once that was the structure he chose to live within, all these other structures grew up beside it. I think the key is that every patriarch engages in denial for the sake of some larger issue.

"Bob is proud of the fact that he's created a world, and when I wrote that novella, I didn't think of it as an Adam myth. I felt I was writing about what it means to be God. This god, Bob, has made his world, and he sees that 'it is good,' but he's made it so completely that there's no opening or niche that his son can call his own."

Bob's "proud to have made it all work in the same way that somebody's proud to be a full professor or to have published novels. He's no more proud than anybody else; he just happens to be more isolated, which gives his pride a certain over-whelming quality. But his child . . . sees that the world is all-encompassing and without any place for him. So I guess what I felt was, that as good as the world is, it belongs to Bob. And what he doesn't understand is that the son wants something for his own even if it's bad."

Smiley believes, and it is clearly part of her philosophical base, that "we all begin our families or our careers in a state of weakness or powerlessness, and the only thing we have is the desire or the ability to make some choice that is a choice of ignorance: 'I haven't dated all the men in the world, but I'm going to choose this guy to spend my life with; I don't really know about all the careers there are, but I'm going to choose this one.' So we start out and we make foolish choices. We can't help but make foolish choices, however they work themselves out.

"I guess," she reflected, "that life is interesting when you feel as though you are in reasonable control, and then something happens that you hadn't forseen, and you spend psychic time, and real time and effort, trying to understand the thing that you hadn't foreseen, whatever it is. While you're trying to understand it, other people around you and life itself demand that you act without having understood what it is you're acting on. There's a lag time between understanding and acting. Acting comes first; understanding comes second. So you find your-self—weeks or months later—down some road where you wouldn't have been if you had been given the time, if you had been able to understand what happened to you. And yet you can't understand what happened to you without having seen how it worked itself out in a kind of dialectic between yourself and the event."

A Thousand Acres, she explains, is also energized by a seemingly inexplicable event. "Something happens, and the daughter to whom it happens feels as though she's putting little pieces together, and yet the ramifications of the event are just outrunning her, and she spends a certain period of time trying to do the right thing, to understand what she should do. But there is no time to do that. And finally, at the end, when disaster has ensued and everything is destroyed, she has to look back and say, 'Well, where did it start?' 'Did it start here?' 'Did it start here?' 'Could I have stopped it?' 'What in me allowed it to go on,' and 'What in my sisters allowed it to go on?'

"To me, that's what all art is about. That's what Shakespeare's about. That's what Sophocles is about. You didn't expect something to happen, and then it happened. And whatever was in you was called forth and was found wanting, and you spend the rest of your life trying to piece back together what it was you should have done, or could have done, or ought to have done, in order to retain what you had before. Except that the thing you had before was an illusory innocence, and you have to say, 'Okay, this thing I had before—which was illusory innocence— would I really want that back, with what I know now?' "

The writer's job, Smiley believes, is to be "energized by the act of understanding," but for her this not does not require isolation. "I have written in restaurants," she said. "I've written sitting with my children as babies, and I think that that furious desire to maintain privacy so that you can write is a male ritual. I would agree with Ursula LeGuin on that score: Often women haven't had space, but there's also something about the family intercourse that energizes their work. That's definitely true of me. Sometimes I'll be in the middle of a sentence and a kid will come in and I'll say, 'Wait a minute until I'm finished with this sentence.' But other times they'll interrupt me anytime. I almost never preserve myself from interruptions because I don't want them to be jealous of my work and it's not really an interruption. My experience is that I can pick up the thread at any time, so why not let them come and talk to me, why not answer the phone, why not? There might be something energizing or interesting happening that you could stick in there."

Smiley is also a teacher and has discovered that teaching creative writing "forces you to theorize about something you are doing instinctively. This used to happen a lot the first five or six years I was teaching. At school I'd say something that I thought was a truism, like there has to be a character transformation in the story. Then I'd come home and I'd reconsider a story that I was having trouble with. I'd see that I wasn't following my own truism, and that's where I was stuck.

"I also have a theory that there are five elements of a story and most stories rely on one or two of them. For example, a thriller relies on suspense, and no matter how great the characterization is or how wonderful the setting is, if the thriller doesn't have enough suspense, the reader will feel that the main promise has been broken. So I try to help my students figure out what elements they're relying on and how to make the story pay off in that element. I just wrote a story that was comic, and part of my theory is that comic stories are almost entirely based in language, which is why the joke lasts five or six lines and then God forbid you have to come up with another one. I found that I was having to go back to it and make the language work better and better and better in a way that I probably wouldn't have done for a more serious story that was relying, say, on character. So teaching gives me a lot of craft-type theory to think about—How do we do this? How do we get from here to here?"

Smiley says that she looks "back on writing a certain book (that other people might see as bleak or depressing) with pleasure at the act of making the phrases or working out the scenes. The readers I love to have are ones that perceive that pleasure and who are willing to understand the sadness or the depressing quality of the material, to gain pleasure from the qualities of the writing," and to "make something of the sad qualities of the book.

"The goal of my characters is a sort of acceptance [of the inexplicable events of life] and what follows [that acceptance] in one's self and one's cohorts and one's friends. My characters never die screaming in rage. They attempt to pull themselves back together and go on. And that's basically a conservative view of life. When you really love a piece of writing that is sad or a downer, your love comes from the fact that you think it's right or just or true that this should happen and that it's been phrased in a right or just or true way. That feeling works against the feeling that, 'Well, it's too bad that this happened to this person.' One time I was taking [the poet] Mark Strand to Iowa City, and we had a terrific laugh because we realized that we both thought all of our books were quite funny, whereas the world thought our books were quite bleak."

Exit, stage right, the midwesterner.

BOOKS BY JANE SMILEY

NOVELS

Barn Blind. New York: Harper & Row, 1980.
At Paradise Gate. New York: Simon & Schuster, 1981;
    Washington Square Press, 1981.
Duplicate Keys. New York: Knopf, 1984.
The Greenlanders. New York: Knopf, 1988; Ivy, 1989.
A Thousand Acres. New York: Knopf, 1991.

SHORT STORIES

The Age of Grief: A Novella and Stories. New York: Knopf, 1987;
    Ivy, 1988.

Ordinary Love and Good Will: Two Novellas. New York: Knopf, 1989; Ivy, 1991.

NONFICTION

Catskill Crafts: Artisans of the Catskill Mountains. New York: Crown, 1987.

Cynthia Kadohata

"I'M SO WIRED! I hardly ever drink coffee," said Cynthia Kadohata, author of *The Floating World,* called *ukiyo* in Japanese, as we sat over one of those four-unusual-sliced-fruits-arranged-on-a-big-plate breakfasts at a Park Avenue hotel. She was in New York just long enough to collect one of ten Mrs. Giles Whiting Foundation Awards for fiction. Then she was planning to rush to the airport in order to fly back to California for her "baby brother's wedding" the next night. Luckily, since she was dressed in a flowered, tie-dyed sarong skirt and a show-stopping, black halter blouse adorned with large wooden beads, she arrived in Manhattan on a particularly warm autumn day.

Kadohata is a second-generation Japanese-American who was born in Chicago and raised in Georgia and Arkansas. Her first novel is the story of Japanese-American "chicken sexers" in Gibson, Arkansas, in 1950s America, who work seventeen-hour shifts (with the help of Dexedrine) identifying male chicks at hatcheries. The males are then drowned, since they do not produce eggs. Like Olivia, her twelve-year-old narrator, "who . . . comes to belong in change, movement, and transition," Kadohata has herself moved repeatedly from one world to another. "I like to travel because it causes me to see ordinary things in a way that surprises me; I can get so used to my surroundings that I stop noticing anything strange about them. Also, traveling erases a vague discomfort or sadness or melancholy or dissatisfaction or something that is frequently with me. Once I was in a sleazy bus station in the middle of nowhere in the middle of the night, and I remember thinking, 'I feel so happy!' Writing and traveling are linked for me in ways I understand and probably in ways that I don't understand as well. But images are often what set me off and make me want to write."

Kadohata was living in Boston when she decided on this career. "I told an editor I knew, 'I want to get better, faster. Should I go to a writing program or not?' He said, 'Well, in general, I think that you can get better, faster, if you go to a program.' He knew there were openings in Pittsburgh, so I went to Pittsburgh, but I didn't feel I was getting better, faster. And then I thought, I've always wanted to live in New York, so I'll apply to Columbia University. I went there and I still didn't feel I was getting better, faster, so I said, 'Forget it. In the old days they used to say that a young writer had to live in New York to establish a career, but you don't have to anymore.' I had read that somewhere and I said, 'I'm leaving.' "

Kadohata "actually liked Pittsburgh better because it seemed less elbows-out competitive, and they seemed friendlier and more supportive. But I don't know. Maybe competitiveness helps too, because there were a couple of writers in Pittsburgh who were very good (and as good as the best writers at Columbia), but they haven't published, and one of them, who was very talented, isn't even writing any more. So maybe that competiveness is part of what you need." In any case, Kadohata is now "very much at home in Los Angeles. It's much more spacious, and you can have more light in your apartment. And there's not the same sort of intense feeling of just being surrounded by publishing.

"Just yesterday, a friend was making fun of me because I used to ask, when I was living in New York, *'Can you really be happy?'* *'Is it good to be happy?'* *'Can you really write if you're not unhappy a little bit, or at least a little bit dissatisfied?'* and he said, now that I've moved to California, that I've started to say, 'I believe in the goodness of life,' and pretty soon I'm going to be getting a personal trainer. Now he calls me a southern California 'girl' writer. My family is out there too, so I feel more comfortable, more at home." [Her father, from whom Kadohata's mother was divorced when the writer was nine, still lives in Springdale, Arkansas, and is a chicken sexer.] And life is apparently so relaxed in California that "a close friend who is a writer said she doesn't want our friendship to be based in publishing, so we don't really talk much about writing." In New York, on the other hand, "you sit at the table and that's all you talk about. You can be with your friends and just hanging out, but you're talking about writing and publishing, it seems. Southern California is a relief. Maybe at some point I'll feel, My God, this is driving me crazy: Nobody reads books! But I haven't felt that yet."

Kadohata's second novel, *In the Heart of the Valley of Love* is set in Los Angeles because "it just made sense there. . . . I don't think I understand anywhere else. Los Angeles is sort of home," even though in *The Floating World* most of the western United States is defined as a place of "gas station attendants, restaurants, and jobs we depended on, the motel towns floating in the middle of fields and mountains."

Like many of the other writers in this book, Cynthia Kadohata is benefiting from the increased interest in the infusion of nonwhite cultures into American society, but suffering from what might be called the misfortune of hyphenization. As Michiko Kakutani wrote in her *New York Times* review of *The Floating World,* the novel "leaves us with a sense of what it means to grow up as part of an immigrant family, what it means to belong to America and yet to stand apart." But Kadohata has strong feelings about being pigeonholed as "a Japanese-American writer; I get mad because they are always very dogmatic about it: 'You have to be [an Asian writer]. . . . Sometimes I want that identity, but not always. . . . When I want to be an Asian writer, then I am one, but I don't like people saying you have to be an Asian writer, and if you do something different, then you're a banana or whatever. I'm reminded of a story a teacher told me. He said he taped two young black men before and after they talked to a white man in a position of authority. Beforehand, when it was just the two of them, they used black English and were articulate and confident, but in the office they used standard English and were inarticulate and awkward. The situation is similar for me, to have to be a Japanese-American writer one day, a woman writer the next, etc. By being each of these things separately, rather than being all of them at once, you disempower yourself, which may be precisely the aim of the people who want you to be only one part of yourself at a time—rather than whole."

Other "hyphenated writers" interviewed for this book recognize that this kind of compartmentalization deprives all readers of a common history and sets historical boundaries that are no advantage for writers of fiction. In Kadohata's case, of course, these boundaries suggest that she should write about America only through Japanese-American eyes. But in discussing *The Floating World,* she maintains that she's "not sure that the Japanese aspect of it would be the main theme. That would be the plot. And I hope my characters are not presented as victims because I don't really like that role. . . . I can't say exactly what I would think the theme is versus the plot: love and life and all of that—and safety."

Her mixed feelings about this struggle for identity "rise from the hostility I might feel if I think about my parents being in [an internment] camp. I'll occasionally feel somewhat hostile, and I'll think, 'Oh . . . that white person over there.' But the hyphenation, Japanese-American, when I choose to use it, is really to say, 'Well, I'm something different and I'm proud of it. I'm separate from what [the other American] are, and what [the other Americans] did."

Is it, I wanted to know, a way of making that memory of Japanese-Americans, and what happened to them during World War II, easier to bear—that someone else did it? "No," Kadohata replied. "It's a little bit pride and a little bit hostility, I would guess."

These conflicts seem more acute since Kadohata moved to the West Coast because "the Asians who live on the West Coast are much more politicized. I didn't even think of all this as an issue until I was on the West Coast." The issues also began to crystallize when Kadohata was surprised and angered by some of the reviews of *The Floating World*. "One, from England, said something like, 'When you look at her picture, she looks Japanese. But when you read the book, the characters are not really Japanese, so what's her problem?'

"Another man who had this radio show in Seattle just attacked me: '*The Floating World* was socially irresponsible. Do Asians really act like this?' " he said. "He was Japanese, and he 'knew the novel wasn't angry enough.' " This radio reviewer, says Kadohata, said that "people like Maxine Hong Kingston and Amy Tan were 'Christian writers,' and I wasn't sure if he was insulting them or not. And he thought I was becoming a part of 'that'." By "that" he apparently meant that Kingston and Tan were writers whose characters, although usually Asian-Americans, were accessible to all readers and too integrated into American experience for his taste. He said, " 'You made the chicken sexers look bizarre.' And I said, 'Well, how did I do that?' And he said, 'Well, I haven't actually read that part of the book, but somebody told me that you did.' "

Kadohata says that this particular radio personality was "a

disciple of Frank Chin [another Asian-American writer], and . . . it is true that some of Frank Chin's group . . . were criticizing certain Asian women writers because they had white hus- bands—even though, of course, Frank Chin has a white wife. But the radio reviewer, I guess, also felt that I didn't talk enough about the camps," which are only peripherally alluded to in the novel. "That's something that came up a lot in interviews and in reviews. Actually, everyone said, 'Why didn't you write more about the camps?' It's funny, because the camps were a very small part of the book. I mean, they were mentioned once or twice. . . . One of the reviews even started talking about the history of the camps! It wasn't in the book, but it was an issue with the reviewer: 'Why didn't Kadohata deal with this?' But that wasn't what the book was about."

Kadohata also remembered "a workshop where somebody said that my characters were not acting Japanese enough, and I didn't know what that meant, eating sushi or something?" What was the workshop director referring to? I wanted to know. "She didn't really say. I guess I had an outburst at that point, so she didn't finish it. I think she just felt that my characters were driving on the road, they were eating in diners, so how were they Japanese if they were doing these things?" There was also "this teacher at Pittsburgh who read a story of mine, and he said, 'Well, you know, this has Japanese characters, but the point of the story is not that they're Japanese. You can't really do that because it's gimmicky.' And I said, 'Why can't you just have Japanese char- acters?' And he said, 'But you have to have a reason for making them Japanese; otherwise they should be white.' And I said, 'That doesn't make sense. Why shouldn't you have a reason for mak- ing them white?' "

Kadohata starts everything she writes by making notes in longhand. "I write on slips of paper, used envelopes, receipts, and then when I feel all those thoughts and details, plans and ideas, coming to a boil, I consolidate and arrange them in a notebook. I try to start typing out the chapter or story as soon as possible, while everything is still boiling, because typing that first draft is the worst part for me. Unlike my friends who write, my favorite part of writing is rewriting. That's the time I feel most in a sort of Zen state (for lack of a better description).

"The other parts of my life that have an impact on my writing are guitar—the lessons require a lot of time and concentration—and my boyfriend, who requires the same. I love him and think he has really helped me find new areas to write about. (Did that come out wrong? I mean, he does have many, many other wonderful qualities that have nothing to do with writing.) But at the same time I don't think I could have gotten published if I'd made my relationships a high priority. I know that's not true for other people, but I feel as if it's better for my writing today to have many important elements in my life, but when I was starting out there was only the writing. I was an obsessed, miserable animal! But it seemed necessary."

Kadohata had just completed *In the Heart of the Valley of Love* when we met in New York. It "takes place in the middle of the twenty-first century and is more about the solutions in society and its possible rebirth. At that point there are more 'minorities' than 'nonminorities.' A friend of mine said that not only in Los Angeles, but all across the country, nonwhites will outnumber whites." In this novel "the [fact that] minorities aren't minorities any more will be taken for granted, and their ethnicity isn't really an issue. It's just there, and it affects things that are happening, but it's not what the book is about." Instead, *In the Heart of the Valley of Love* is the story of seventeen-year-old Rachel, who arrives in "the valley of love" and ends up staying seven years: "During that time," Rachel recalls, "I went to college, fell in and out of love twice with the same man, and failed, many times, not in classes, but in other, more personal ways."

Kadohata says that when she made the decision to have the details of the story occur "in the future, they seemed to take on a more surreal aspect, but I also wanted it to seem very real, like it could happen." When I asked for an example, Kadohata mentioned "ideas about what it means to be white or nonwhite. And it's not like everybody has a particular idea, or everybody has the same idea, but everybody thinks about race and ethnicity, and if it's set in the future, maybe you won't look at it in the same way. At the end you don't know what's going to happen. There's about to be, not exactly a revolution, but sort of mass rioting, and the character has decided that she's going to stay in Los Angeles rather than try to leave."

I wondered whether Kadohata had considered sidetracking the whole issue of ethnicity by using non-Asian characters and setting a book in Indiana, for instance. "I might put the Asian characters in Indiana. But I think it would be important to me to have the characters be Asian, . . . even if they're acting exactly the way they would be acting if they were non-Asian," as they do in *The Floating World* in those drives across the Pacific Northwest made by Olivia's family—three brothers, her grandmother, her mother, and stepfather, Charlie-O, a sweet-tempered gambler. "I just feel there would have to be Asian characters in anything I write, even if the only thing I do that is Asian is to call the character Fumiko."

She is also making peace with the inevitable comparisons to Amy Tan, who is Chinese-American, and to other Asian writers. "It was funny. Last spring I was at a book party, . . . and two people came up to me at the party and said, 'Oh, somebody told me you were Amy Tan!' 'No, I'm not,'" said Kadohata. "And then somebody was talking about my book, and they said, 'Well, in Amy Tan's book' . . . They are always comparing what you do to what Amy Tan does because she is the most prominent Asian writer right now. Even my dad will call me up and say, 'Hey, Amy Tan did this. Why don't you?' and I have to say, 'Dad, leave me alone.'

"It's weird, because when I see Gish Jen [the author of *Typical American*, also a Chinese-American] doing well, I think, 'Go, Gish.' But, at the same time, I don't want people saying, 'Gish did this' and 'How do you feel about Gish?' all the time just because she's Asian." But, she added, "in my heart I do feel that sistership."

In spite of the fact that Cynthia Kadohata was not writing a book specifically about Japanese-Americans, themes of racial tension and ethnicity permeate *The Floating World,* which Kadohata originally planned to call *Seven Moons,* after those lunar phases that mark the passage of time. In *The Floating World,* Olivia Osaka's cigar-smoking grandmother, Obasan, who has outlived three husbands and seven lovers, tells her granddaughter to " 'Smile at them. . . .' *Hakujin* (white people) don't know when a smile is an insult.' She always said her experience showed that if you hated white people, they would just hate you back and nothing would change in the world; and if you didn't hate them after the way they treated you, you would end up hating yourself, and nothing would change that way either. So it was no good not to hate them. So nothing changed."

Kadohata ended the interview by telling me, somewhat hesitantly, "about an old teacher of mine who was very nice to me and very encouraging. But when I first got published, she said to a group of her students, 'Of course it's just because she's a minority.' It got back to me because she said this in front of somebody who *is* actually a good friend of mine, and I felt betrayed. I had thought she was really a great teacher. But maybe it was just a writerly thing. If she didn't say that, she'd say something else, like, 'She knows that editor,' or the usual thing, which someone else asked me: 'Who did you have to fuck to get published?'

In other words, this is no business for babies. Or, as grandmother Obasan says to Olivia in *The Floating World,* "Watch out for life. . . . It's harder than it looks."

BOOKS BY CYNTHIA KADOHATA

NOVELS

The Floating World. New York: Viking, 1989; Ballantine, 1991.
In the Heart of the Valley of Love. New York: Viking, 1992.

Terry Tempest Williams

NEWSWEEK recently called the soft-spoken, intensely private Terry Tempest Williams one of those people most likely to have "a considerable impact on the political, economic, and environmental issues facing the western states in this decade." Williams, naturalist-in-residence at the Utah Museum of Natural History, fifth-generation Mormon woman, former teacher on the Navajo reservation at Montezuma Creek, and ardent environmentalist who lives with her husband, Brooke, among the wildflowers of Emigration Canyon, is now, in addition to all of the above, a public person—one of the "new voices of the West."

Her most recent book, *Refuge—An Unnatural History of Family and Place,* best described as part memoir and part love song to her spiritual home, the Bear River Migratory Bird Refuge on Great Salt Lake, perfectly positions her for this role. As Wallace Stegner has noted, it chronicles how "the extravagant bird life of the marshes dwindles and all but disappears before the rising tide of salt water as the women of the Tempest-Romney families—two grandmothers, a mother, six aunts, Terry Tempest Williams herself—wilt before the inexorable invasion of disease." The rise of Great Salt Lake in the 1980s and the resulting flooding of her beloved bird sanctuary serve as counterpoint for the story of her family as it is battered by cancer.

Williams, however, says that she wrote *Refuge* (begun when she was twenty-eight years old and completed at thirty-five) "to remember my mother and grandmothers and what it was that we shared, and as a way of recalling how women conduct their lives in the midst of family, in the midst of illness, in the midst of death—in the midst of day-to-day living. I wrote *Refuge* to celebrate the correspondence between the landscape of my childhood and the landscape of my family, to explore the idea of how one finds refuge in change. And it is *Refuge* that gave me my voice as a woman."

She wanted "to explore the idea of what the language that women speak would really be if no one were there to correct them," as Hélène Cixous has challenged. The links between women, embedded in language, she realized, are the seeds of legacy. "And the essential element of legacy," said Williams, "is story, the umbilical cord that connects the past, present, and future. When you tell a story it's as though a third person has entered the room, and you become accountable for that sacred knowledge: Story binds us to community. Part of the reason I could write *Refuge,* which is so intensely personal, is my belief that inside story the personal is transformed into the general, the universal. Story becomes the conscience of our communities."

Williams says, "The language that women speak when no one is there to correct them is the language of the heart, a kin to the land." She goes on to say, "Women's language is like connective tissue, detailed and circuitous; it goes in and out. When two women speak, they can keep five strands of conversation going at once—getting back to here, getting back to there. It drives my father crazy. He says, 'So, what's the bottom line? What are you really trying to say?'

"I'm always aware when I'm not speaking my own language that there is a time restraint placed on me, that I have to say so much in x-amount of time or else the [male listener's] concentration will be gone. But the language of women knows no time. A woman's language is about meanderings, like a river: You may go through eddies and spiral in one place again and again. You may enter white water, full of risk and danger. . . . You may just decide to take the flat water very slowly. It is language without self-consciousness.

"I love Claudia Herrmann's book, *The Tongue Snatchers,* when she says that [women] literally are a species in translation, that the language as it is defined by the dominant culture today is not the mother tongue. So I am interested, as a writer, in finding what the mother tongue *is.* I believe it has to do with structure, form, and style. I think it has to do with identifying relationships that break through the veneer of what is proper, what is expected. The language that women speak when nobody is there to correct them oftentimes can make people uncomfortable because it threatens to undermine the status quo. It's what we know in our hearts that we don't dare speak, . . . the sense of women and secrets."

Williams's love of story seems to be related to her identification as a Mormon, a member of the Church of Jesus Christ of Latter-Day Saints. Although she says that the reaction to *Refuge* in her religious community has been "mixed," and "many of my relatives and extended family have been somewhat disturbed by the book because they feel that I betrayed secrets in the family and death should be private," she also points out that "as a Mormon, at a very early age you are encouraged to tell your story. One of the great traditions in Mormon religion is Testimony Meeting. For two hours, usually the first Sunday of each month, everyone sits inside the chapel and, when so moved, you rise and tell your story. It doesn't matter if you've had a personal vision or if you just want to stand up and thank Sister Young for the casserole she brought over when you were sick." This kind of storytelling "is a time for the community to share their spiritual experiences for the past month. I remember standing up at a very early age and bearing my testimony of God—I had planted tulip bulbs in the fall with my mother and in the spring watched them bloom. I believed in the Resurrection because of perennials. That was my story. I sat down and I was showered with support. In Mormon culture, I was taught to value my own experience."

When Terry Tempest Williams wrote in *Refuge,* "In Mormon culture, authority is respected and independent thinking is not, . . ." she realized that she was going against the current of Mormon theology. "My point was that for me the price of obedience was too high. We must think for ourselves and act out of our own instincts, not out of a patriarchal mandate. . . . There were people who were uncomfortable when I suggested that the Holy Ghost might be a feminine presence, when I said I pray to a Heavenly Mother as well as a Heavenly Father and that, ultimately, I pray to the birds." For her community that was "paganism. . . . All these things were controversial on some level. The fact that women give each other blessings is something that every Mormon woman knows, but we don't share, so in speaking the unspeakable you have violated some sort of trust. But I don't feel that way because [the language of women] goes beyond Mormonism. If we are going to move forward with any sort of compassionate intelligence, it is going to be the strength of women that provides us with a lifeline. . . . There has been a positive response from the Mormon hierarchy of women because they see in this book the values of family and community and prayer and faith that are all honored within the Mormon tradition."

Williams "grew up in a pretty free home" with "a high threshold of guilt, although my mother and father were very strong members of the Church. But there was also a kind of renegade spirit. We knew that our relationship to the land was our relationship to each other. We could hold Church in the middle of the Great Basin as well as in the Monument Park Fourteenth Ward. My paternal grandmother, Kathryn Blackett Tempest ("Mimi"), was a modern-day shaman—if you dare say that without regard to New Age connotations. Here she was, having nightly visions in her dreams. She would call us up and ask, "Did you dream last night? And what was it, dear?" Our dreams had power because our grandmother valued them. She would look up the images in Carl Jung's *Man and His Symbols,* J. E. Cirlot's *Dictionary of Symbols,* and in *The Golden Bough,* so as children of six, seven, and eight years old, she was teaching us that our dreams count. In my mind that was about 'free agency.' We could choose to remember our dreams or we could choose to forget them. If we chose to forget them, we were ignoring the language of the soul."

Williams's father, John Tempest, is "the quintessential Marlboro man, who has always been extremely independent. I mean, I didn't know that men had feet. I thought they had cowboy boots. So there was this rugged individualism, embodied in the men in my family, that really is a stereotype of the American West and that too is about 'free agency,' a tenet within Mormonism. Since my grandfather, Jack Tempest, whom we loved dearly, was not a member of the Church, I just dismissed the idea that only Mormons go to heaven, since that precluded him. I thought as a child, 'Obviously, they've got that one wrong.' My other grandparents, Lettie and Sanky Dixon, didn't live by the letter of the law, but by the spirit of the law, and that also supported my idea of individual freedom within orthodoxy.

"At an early age, because of my extended family of four grandparents and five great-grandparents, my history was alive around our dinner table. My great-grandmother, Vilate Romney, would say, "Remember who you are, the pioneer stock you come from." The message was clear, we could choose how we wanted to live our lives, we were intelligent women, we were a strong family, and we could endure whatever came our way. We had the intellectual and spiritual freedom to move within the structure. Although an orthodox Mormon may think free agency is about honoring obedience and finding freedom within that obedience, spiritual laws and principles, I've never honored that belief. For me, the most important value is independent thought, the freedom to choose a creative path. That's how I have been able to survive within the Mormon tradition."

Terry Tempest Williams has herself survived two nonmalignant breast tumors, and she is able to write and speak about the impact of disease in her life. "In the spring of 1983, when my mother, Diane Tempest, was diagnosed with ovarian cancer, I kept vigil for weeks in the hospital. My mother was hinting that a bit of privacy would be nice, and I remember her saying that people in hospitals can be pale, but their family members cannot be. I took her cue and drove out to the bird refuge, where I have always found solace. I remember getting out of my car and walking out toward the marsh I had always counted on. With water lapping around my ankles, the flooding Great Salt Lake, I realized devastation knows no boundaries. The landscape of my childhood and the landscape of my family—the two things I had always regarded as bedrock—were now subject to change. That's when the story began. That's when my search began. There was really nothing extraordinary about it. It was a family moving through illness together, and it was the juxtaposition of being with my mother, being with the birds that allowed me to discover the story that was there.

"In terms of legacy and the idea that memory is the only way home, I don't think we can really ever know what we've been through, or what we've experienced, or how we have changed, unless we use memory as a tool for reflection. There were many layers to uncover in the writing of *Refuge*: the actual living of it, the recording of it in my journals, and then letting the whole story steep like a hot cup of tea. Then I had to get it down on paper in a nonperfunctory way (which is very difficult in itself), really being tied to the chronology—the lake levels, the dates my mother became ill, and when the recurrence came—literally making an outline of time. And then I had to go back and let it all go—I had to say, 'What are the ideas here? What is the essence here? What are the universalities? And what is my place within this story? Where is my narrative apart from my mother's and grandmother's stories?' It became intensely difficult because in a sense, I was dealing with major taboos—mother and daughter relationships, the voice of the feminine, and of course, death. It was the unmasking of these deep archetypes, and it was not without its pain.

"Death," she mused, "is an abstraction and a mystery. You can never really know what death is, particularly in our society, since we have such little experience with death. We turn it over to someone else, we abrogate our responsibility, and death becomes something that takes place in hospitals behind closed doors. It is antiseptic. Someone else takes care of it, and we tend to move in and out with great fear and trepidation. My mother didn't allow for that. She insisted that we move through the landscape of grief with her, that her death would be a conscious death. In a strange sort of way, in the midst of the heartache and suffering, there was a sense of adventure. Particularly, the last month when she was dying, I remember driving down the canyon thinking, 'I wonder what I am going to learn today. . . .' My mother believed that you could not only live well, but you could die well.

"I remember going to our local bookstore and ordering every book I could get my hands on: Elisabeth Kübler-Ross's *On Death and Dying*, Stephen Levine's, *Who Dies?* I must have had a dozen or more books to pick up. The woman behind the counter looked at me with great tenderness. Finally, as I went to pay for them, she took my hand, shook her head, and said, "I just don't know what to say." My idea was, if this is the territory we are about to enter, let us be as well informed as possible. Ultimately, what I have discovered is that each death is individual. There are no rules. And I still have no sense of what death really is except to say, I believe it is a process, akin to birth, and that even now, after my mother and grandmothers are dead, the relationships continue."

Death is "about subtleties, and I think [that's] what propels us in life to be courageous, to take nothing for granted. And there is this whole business of the flesh. I recall walking through the desert in southern Utah and coming upon the carcass of a deer. I thought, that might be the most disturbing aspect of all—not death but the decomposition of life—that we are never allowed to see. The deterioration of our bodies, of those we love, is hidden from us. We are embalmed, the mortician takes over. It all looks so nice."

It was also interesting to talk to Terry Tempest Williams, a woman fascinated with birds, about the mother-daughter relationship, because it turns out that her "mother was really uncomfortable with birds. I think her sense of birds was along the lines of Tippi Hedren in Alfred Hitchcock's film. But she did have a strong sense of the natural world and of spiritual things, and that's where she went to find her refuge. She believed that the natural world was the third partner in her marriage. And I love that mothers and daughters can be different, that they don't have to be the same, that those differences can provide a creative tension, growth."

It was her paternal grandmother, Mimi, Williams said, "who allowed my mother and me to have a very pure relationship even though we were so different. I was a very intense child. Mother had three other children and a demanding husband, along with church duties." Mimi turned her intensity into creative outlets. "Mimi would put on music and we'd dance around the living room. I remember the way she would set up an easel, and we would paint to the music when we would tire of dance. We would spend endless hours getting up before dawn, waiting for the first light to strike, so we could see what birds were there.

And we would be still. I remember sitting in an aspen grove with her and she'd say, 'Let us be patient. The gift of the natural world comes to those who wait.' It was in those moments together as women that I learned to be myself. There was no censoring; there was no editing; there was intrinsic trust."

When I interviewed Terry Tempest Williams she had recently given a series of readings at bookstores across the West and she was both physically and emotionally exhausted, primarily from identifying with the stories of audience members. Williams said softly that she "wasn't prepared for that. . . . What I found in sharing *Refuge* and in giving readings was the yearning we have to belong to a community, the yearning we have to share our stories. We are told a story and then we tell our own. Our lives are so fast-paced right now, there is no time to indulge ourselves in grief. And in my mind, it is not an indulgence, it is a necessity. Grief takes time and you have to sit with it, embrace it. And there are times when you are immobilized by it. But that is part of the process. It is that 'laziness of grief' that C. S. Lewis writes about, where to even pick up a pen to write a letter is the ordeal of the day. You need to be left alone with it. I think for one year I simply stared out the window. Not really, but that's what it felt like, a melancholy trance. Since we don't allow ourselves the time, or in reality don't have it, when someone dies, we bury them and are back to business as usual the next day. Our grief is repressed, and then there's something amiss in our lives, and we hardly even know what it is. In this sense, I think, *Refuge* has given people an occasion to cry, an occasion to feel. And that is because this story is not uncommon—the death of a loved one is universal.

"It's been very moving to listen to people's stories, particularly about cancer, because cancer is a transformative disease and the grace of cancer is that you can be in the presence of death. The opportunity of cancer, a disease that is literally racking the body, is that, in the midst of the pain, you can have a conscious death." Williams realizes that "cancer may, in fact, be in my genes. . . . I can't say that I look forward to death. In a very real sense, I fight every day to live. But one of the things I've learned since my mother was first diagnosed with breast cancer (I was fifteen years old) is that all you really have is the day at hand. I guess I don't really believe death exists in the conventional sense because when I was with my mother and grandmothers, it was like a moment of birth—transformation—life as a continuous state of being—movement—energy. What I have come to value and love most about the natural world is this same kind of regenerative spirit."

All of these themes resonate in *Refuge,* and Williams says that the reviewers have displayed "some frustration. You know, 'What is this book about? Is it about birds? Is it about Bear River? Is it about Great Salt Lake? Is it about Mormonism? Is it about women? Is it about nuclear testing? . . . Give us the point!' In one of the reviews, *Library Journal,* a reviewer states, 'This book is difficult to categorize; I don't know where I would put it on the shelf.' But life cannot be so easily compartmentalized; it is all woven together. When I wrote *Pieces of White Shell—A Journey to Nava-joland,* I think I found it in every section in bookstores except 'whimsy.'

"I think we have to write out of the integrity of our own vision, and I am aware that borders are fluid not fixed, that we have to chart our own territory as we write out of the truth of our lives." In this context, Williams mentioned the work of Louise Erdrich and Ursula LeGuin. "I don't think women are so easily pigeonholed in a particular genre. We are just writing out of the passion of our own experience. We are taught not to trust our own experience, but experience is all we have."

She has also been influenced in various ways by *The Book of Mormon,* which she says "has taught me the power of story because really *The Book of Mormon* is one story after another. It has taught me the power of a homeland, that place matters to a people, that each individual is entitled to [his or her] own personal vision. I was raised in a religion that says: Joseph Smith had a question. He went to a sacred grove of trees and fell to his knees in prayer. God appeared and counseled him to start his own religion. That's pretty powerful doctrine for a child. What it said to me was that each of us is entitled to his or her own spiritual quest, and that your answer may not be the same answer as your neighbor's but each has credence. That may not be what my Mormon Elders hoped I would learn from our sacred texts, but that's what I have taken for myself. I think that's why in *Refuge* when I say, 'I pray to the birds, . . .' I am really saying I find my spirituality in the connectedness of *all* life. Everything is endowed with its own spirit. I was taught there was a spirit world that was created before this Earth and that it exists now, and therefore all life is sacred.

"What I am interested in are the questions. In *Pieces of White Shell,* it was, What stories do we tell that evoke a sense of place? In *Refuge,* it was, How do we find refuge in change? And with [her current subject] eroticism, I want to know how an intimacy with the land can enable us to embrace an intimacy with ourselves or, more to the point, how a lack of intimacy with the land leads to a lack of intimacy with each other. Again, this is about taboos and taking off the masks. Sensuality is a taboo. Since we don't talk about our bodies, I'm interested in writing out of the body, the body of the Earth, and what that form might take regarding language and story. I want to see how we might redefine the erotic, how an erotics of place might lead to a politics of place. Ultimately, it's about the love we fear. We are so afraid of loving the Earth, loving each other, loving ourselves.

"I think an erotics of place may be one of the reasons why environmentalists are seen as subversive. There is a backlash now: . . . take all the regulations away; weaken existing legislation; the endangered species act is too severe, too restrictive; let there be carte blanche for real-estate developers. Because if we really have to confront wildness, solitude, and serenity, both the fierceness and compassionate nature of the land, then we ultimately have to confront it in ourselves, and it's easier to be numb, to be distracted, to be disengaged. There is so much self-loathing, the constant doubting of what we can do, not trusting our own instincts, our own experience, our own goodness and power.

Our culture of consumerism tells us what we need, what we want, and what we deserve. It is the economics of entitlement. And I believe it is an illusion. I believe our needs are more basic: home; family; community; health; the health of the land which includes all life forms, plants, animals, and human beings. We need open country, open spaces, a wildness that offers us deliverance from inauthentic lives."

Terry Tempest Williams is "deeply committed as a writer and as a woman to a politics of place." She says, "We can transform the world through story. I write out of my life. And when Hélène Cixous says, 'I-woman am going to blow up the Law. . . . Let it be done, right now, *in* language, . . .' I believe her. I have made a personal commitment to stop nuclear testing. My pen is my weapon, and as an act of hope or ritual, I choose to cross the line and commit civil disobedience. Our family, and so many others in Utah, are downwinders. This spring, there is going to be a huge action, called 'The Hundredth Monkey,' at the Nevada test site. I will be there in the name of my mother and grandmothers, members of the Clan of One-Breasted Women. You do what you can on whatever level you can, and you do what you do best. And by the power of our own minds and our own hearts, we can write the world. This is about passion and presence." And, she adds, "Our obligation as writers is to make people uncomfortable, to push the borders of what is possible."

Even though Williams has already endured the loss of seven family members from cancer, and the disruption of her own refuge, she feels that "there is a place of peace—even if it's a square foot of an empty lot, a garden, or the sky at night. There is something beyond which will hold us in all of life's ambiguity. I choose to court the mysteries. I don't think there is such a thing as security, but I know my home and I know my land, and as long as I live, I will stand my ground in the places I love."

"The birds have simply moved on," she says. "They give me the courage to do the same."

BOOKS BY TERRY TEMPEST WILLIAMS

NONFICTION

Coyote's Canyon. Salt Lake City: Peregrine Smith Books, 1989.
Pieces of White Shell: A Journey to Navajoland. New York: Scribner, 1984.
Refuge: An Unnatural History of Family and Place. New York:
    Pantheon, 1991.

Jessica Hagedorn

JESSICA HAGEDORN lives in the jail near Charles Street in lower Manhattan.

To be precise, the Filipino-American poet, performance artist, and author of *Dogeaters,* which was nominated for the National Book Award in 1990, lived, at the time of our interview, in the "old [two-story] holding cells," behind the Sixth Police Precinct, which is itself now a popular rental apartment building. Hagedorn, who at forty-one was then pregnant with her second daughter, met me near the elevators; we wound our way through a maze of basement hallways and out to a geranium-filled courtyard that separated the former police station from her front door.

Jessica Hagedorn's apartment consisted of one room about ten feet wide, plus a minute kitchen housed in a former closet that was bracketed by turquoise bookcases. On the living room wall hung a blowup of a Steve Canyon comic strip that said: "It's simple, Steve. Why don't you and your boys just get the fuck out of El Salvador?" A steep and narrow staircase (lined with "kitchy representations of the Virgin") led to a loft bedroom and a closet which had been transformed into a small child's bedroom. Unhappily, because this apartment was indeed an artist's delight, there was not one foot of available space for the expected baby's crib, so Hagedorn, her Chinese-American husband (a film designer and producer), and their two daughters moved recently to a larger apartment in this neighborhood of artists, musicians, and writers.

Although she was born in the Philippines and moved to the San Francisco Bay area at the age of fourteen, where she was educated at the American Conservatory Theater, Hagedorn has now lived in the United States for more than twenty years and in New York City's Greenwich Village for twelve years. Like many New Yorkers, she ended up here almost by mistake. Although she had badgered her parents since she "was nine or ten to send me to acting school and loved the idea of [acting] five days a week," since she did not fit the stereotype of the blonde, all-American heroine, Hagedorn realized that she "wasn't interested in running around auditioning for parts as hookers. I thought, 'I'm never going to play big roles; it's ridiculous. But I can write, and I can create worlds.' "

After her first book of poetry, *Dangerous Music,* was published in 1975, she started working with musicians in San Francisco and formed a poets' band. "We were sort of a novelty," Hagedorn explained, "because we wanted to combine words and music and not have it be boring or stuffy." She "would invite people to come in and sort of do anarchistic little . . . things in the middle of a song or something," a technique that later became known as "performance art." Her band, the West Coast Gangster Choir, was successful, and Hagedorn was invited "to do a bunch of readings in New York with two very close friends, Thulani Davis and Ntozake Shange, who had moved back here from San Francisco to develop [what] later became *for colored girls who have considered suicide / when the rainbow is enuf*. We had this reading at an uptown bar for women, the Sahara, and we decided to do it with Anthony Davis, a jazz musician who later composed the opera *X [The Life and Times of Malcolm X]*. It went very well. Joe Papp [then director of New York's Public Theater] came to see us. He had a cabaret show at the Public Theater, and he wanted us to be part of it. 'When?' " Hagedorn asked. "And he said, 'In a couple of weeks; we have to go into rehearsal right away.' And I had, like, one little bag and it was winter here. I remember this very clearly, and I was completely unprepared. But of course we all said 'Yes,' and our lives went upside down. . . . I borrowed clothes and I just stayed and stayed. This was 1978. The show ran for four months and finally I went back to California, packed up my stuff, sold everything that I couldn't put in a bag, and decided I'd try New York."

Papp was apparently so impressed that "he asked me if I wanted to do my own show [called "Mango Tango"] as a workshop production for a few weeks, so of course I said, 'Yes.' " But she did not continue to pursue this career as performance artist until her "old guitar player showed up in New York and said, 'Let's put a band together.' I was sort of scared because the punk scene was happening then and I thought, 'Could we compete with all that? It's too much; I don't know if we can cut it,' but he really wanted to jump into it, so I thought, 'Why not?' " Hagedorn says that "part of the reason I had the band [for ten years, until 1985] is because I wanted my poetry to reach people who think poetry is boring. I don't blame them; I hated poetry in school, and I thought it was taught like some dead thing. If people don't like it, I can see why they don't."

Her involvement with performance art now seems to have

given way permanently to writing fiction. "I wanted to write *Dogeaters* and finish it, and I knew I couldn't do [both], so I made a choice." She returned to the Philippines in 1988 because "it was part of my mission to go back and spend a few months and get the book done. I got completely reinspired: . . . The way people talked and the food, it was all there, even the smell. It was great."

This reintroduction to the elements of popular culture that often define a country seems especially important to Hagedorn because, like many of the artists in her particular expatriate's community, she feels "really psychically connected to the Philippines"; and her reinvolvement with the food of her native country was especially crucial. No one could read *Dogeaters* and fail to notice the "minced red salted duck eggs dabbed with vinegar," "shrimp wrapped in taro leaves, stewed in a mixture of hot chili and coconut milk," "peppery sweet *lechon kawali,* grilled *bangus,*" and ". . . a *pinakbet* with bitter-melon, squash, okra, and string beans stewed with cloves of garlic, bits of pork fat, and salty fermented shrimp *bagoong,*" or the "scrambled eggs over garlic-fried rice, side of longaniza sausages, and beef *tapa.*" In all the chapters, Filipino food is elaborately discussed because "food really captures the Filipino culture. I have that speech the Senator gives: 'Food is the center of our ritual celebrations, our baptisms, weddings, funerals.' Those are my true feelings about the culture I grew up in. You can't describe a real Pinoy [Filippino] without listing what's most important to him—food, music, dancing, and love—most probably in that order, and I think it's true of most cultures where food is very important and where celebrations are centered around food." But, in the Philippines, Hagedorn says, "even the poorest of the poor will offer you their last bowl of rice, and you should take it, because it would really hurt if you didn't. I think, on some level, that's a very beautiful aspect of the culture, and on another level within this story I wove in *Dogeaters,* the food is also used to hide what's going on: I mean, 'Let's not talk about it; let's eat.'"

These are "things I've observed in my own family, for example.

The food takes precedence because we can all relate to that: It's delicious and wonderful." Offering people food, Hagedorn recalls, "is part of a hospitality that's deeply ingrained in the culture. It's beautiful, but at the same time I think that's the reason the culture was so easily exploited."

According to Hagedorn, the New York Times reviewer pointed out that " 'everybody's hungering for something' " in Dogeaters. "I mean, that's the truth, that was a conscious metaphor for me. There is a chapter that I call 'Hunger,' as a matter of fact. Everyone is hungry! It's a culture where everyone is very hungry to find themselves, to get out of this trap of oppression, and there are no answers. I had no answers for it."

This dilemma resonates in the novel because all of the characters seem to lack collective histories, although Hagedorn strives mightily to endow each character with a personal biography. The characters are so in love with the idea of make-believe that both the individual and collective histories seem instead to be movie stories. This is true particularly of the male prostitute, Joey, a junkie and an orphan ("I love Joey; he's my favorite character"), who is "certainly oppressed by society and self-oppressed." Joey, the son of a black American soldier and a beautiful whore, Zenaida, who drowned herself when he was small, was sold to a small-time crook named "Uncle," and his sordid life consists of his obsessions with food and sexual tradeoffs. In fact, the sense in this novel is that most of the characters, not only Joey, are disposable people and emotional orphans. Hagedorn seemed to agree with this: "Emotional orphans is a good term, but I also feel that they are real survivors." And she is sensitive to the response her novel and these kinds of characterizations have elicited from the emigré Filipino community. "I've gotten in a lot of hot water with certain segments, . . . who were horrified by the title [an ethnic slur for Filipinos] and with bringing out all the dirty laundry, which was something I prepared myself for. But when it happens, you still get hurt. A lot of them hadn't even read the book; they just made all these assumptions."

I asked Hagedorn why the characters in Dogeaters—Rio Gonzaga and her buxom cousin Pucha, privileged school girls who spend boring days watching Rock Hudson movies, Rio's maternal grandmother, Lola Narcisa, and her paternal grandmother, Abuelita Socorro (who wears a scrap of the Shroud of Turin pinned to her brassiere)—all seem to be adrift and, at the same time, trapped. Her answer was that Filipinos are trapped "because of being colonized. The Philippines was an artificial society that was put together by the Spaniards, you know. They claimed all these [7,100] islands in the southwest Pacific, and a lot of these tribes had nothing to do with each other. Then they lumped them all together and said, *"It's the Philippines!"* For hundreds of years they've been under someone else's rule, and now we have all these strange borders and we all have to get together. But if left to their own devices, none of the tribes would have gotten together anyway, so the problem is ongoing. It hasn't stopped, even with so-called independence, because they're always sort of looking to the West to bail them out of situations, and this dependence has created a really vicious cycle. . . . We don't know who we are, and we have to find our own voices. That's something we are going to be grappling with for a long time.

"As I live here in this country, I often wonder what shaped my imagination: Movies did, and certainly the things I read, and the Church. . . . I think the Catholic Church has had, whether I like it or not, a real impact on me, and I think I finally learned how to use it because . . . it's a rich treasure chest of visual imagery." Hagedorn admitted that "there's a whole period [in a person's life] when you can say, 'Fuck the Church,' and then, you know, you get in your forties and it becomes, like, death is around the corner, and you start wondering, What does life mean?" For these reasons, her daughter Paloma was "baptized in St. Mark's Episcopal Church. It's a poet's church, and the minister there, David Garcia, is very radical. His baptismal service was in part about liberation theology and the problems in Nicaragua. And I like that. It was immediate and not abstract. It's interesting for me to have to grapple with giving Paloma a sense of something bigger than herself, without all the creepy stuff that organized religion lays on you, because I don't want her to have to suffer through that. But I also think that without some kind of moral tissue or spirituality life is very empty."

This belief is clear in *Dogeaters,* with its profuse religious imagery, and Hagedorn admits that she doesn't "think I could have written this book without all of this [background in Catholicism]." Filipinos, she says, "love that religion because it fits in with the melodramatic nature of our national character. That's why I think Catholicism—not just any kind of Christianity—had to be the dominant religion. The Spanish idea of, 'bring on the cross,' really caught on because it was so full of pageantry. It captured the passion and the suffering of the Filipino people."

The religiosity of the culture in *Dogeaters* is in marked contrast, however, with the scenes of corrupt sexuality, particularly the descriptions of bars with homosexual "shower dancers" who soap *up* (to James Brown's song "Sex Machine") as erotic entertainment for the audience. "That was so shocking to me," Hagedorn said. "All that started happening after I grew up." When Hagedorn was a child, Filipino society "was very repressed sexually and, by the time I left, martial law had come in, but I started hearing all this stuff about how there was this underground industry of pornographic shows and sex tours, and I thought, Really? Not that things like that weren't going on [earlier] on a small scale, but the fact that we were so Catholic, . . . [the contrast] was bizarre.

"It was a thriving industry and it still is. . . . I went back a lot during martial law because I missed my family in Manila, I was living in San Francisco, I was single, and it was cheaper to fly there from the West Coast. Sometimes I would go back twice a year and say, What is this? It was horrible to me, the depths of depravity that people had sunk to, but I knew why: They had to make a living. The hypocrisy surfaces in a code of censorship that's upheld: The movies have to be very sanitized, but the government was supporting this porno [film] industry that only people in the know could go to." Hagedorn pointed out that the scene where Lolita Luna, a character in *Dogeaters,* who is a sexy movie star and the mistress of a rich and powerful general, is approached "is based on fact. Famous actors in the Philippines would be tempted to make porno films for a lot of money; you could call the whole thing 'celebrity pornography.' Live sex shows, on the other hand, were for tourists. Sailors would go to bars, which is a whole different scene. All of it was too expensive for the average Filipino."

I asked Hagedorn if, like many writers born in another country, she thought of herself as a "hyphenated" American. "I don't feel like I'm a plain, ordinary American, but I don't know what that is [either]," and "I don't know how to get around the heavy verbiage, . . . so many things to explain who you are. I hate all this. But in a way I think that kind of transition is something we need to do. Until I was fourteen, I was speaking English and Spanish with Tagalog [pronounced ta-gal'-ug] mixed in," as many of her characters do. (Tagalog is an Indonesion language, the chief native language of the Philippine Islands.) "The school I went to was taught in English although we had to have a class in formal Tagalog, which is very deep and very difficult and hardly anybody in Manila speaks it well. And it's interesting to me that I didn't forget it, because I've forgotten a lot of the Spanish, and you'd think in this country I'd have more room to speak Spanish than Tagalog. But the Tagalog stayed."

These questions of identity and of identification are obviously issues that Jessica Hagedorn thinks about. So I asked if she was afraid of being labeled as "the Filipino writer." "I wouldn't care," she said. "I write what I want to write. But I don't necessarily want to write another book about the Philippines." However, she continued, "if my characters happen to be Filipino, and they have to go back and forth because that's where the story takes them, it's fine with me. And if people read that as being, 'Oh, she's the *Filipino* writer,' I don't care. . . . It's, like, not my problem.' "

Right.

BOOKS BY JESSICA (TARAHATA) HAGEDORN

POETRY / SHORT FICTION

Dangerous Music. San Francisco: Momo's Press, 1975.
Pet Food and Tropical Apparitions. San Francisco: Momo's Press, 1981.

NOVELS

Dogeaters. New York: Pantheon, 1990; Penguin, 1991.

MULTIMEDIA THEATER PIECES (UNPUBLISHED)

"Holy Food," n.d.
"Teeny Town," n.d.
"Mango Tango," n.d.

Shirley Abbott

PICTURE two women—one New Yorker and one from New Jersey—sitting in the office of the *University of California at Berkeley Wellness Letter,* a cheery place with hanging plants and exposed brick walls on traffic-clogged, lower Broadway in New York City, and reminiscing about their childhood adventures in, of all places, Hot Springs, Arkansas. Even when nothing could have prepared you for this specific connection, it quickly becomes a metaphor for the ways in which women's lives, and their memories, so often overlap and interweave.

The New Yorker in this case, Shirley Abbott (actually Shirley Jean, named for *The Good Ship Lollipop* princess), is the author of *Womenfolks: Growing Up Down South* and recently of *The Bookmaker's Daughter,* which was reviewed nationwide, including on the front page of the *New York Times Book Review*. Abbott grew up in the town "without a lid," a place of therapeutic mineral waters and steamy bathhouses, where illegal betting parlors attracted, among others, Al Capone from Chicago and the pool-playing hustler, Minnesota Fats. The main street of Hot Springs was lined with gaudy auction houses where visitors hoped to "find the Hope diamond or *the* Oriental carpet and get it for cheap." Hot Springs was a place where miracles were the main product.

Now in her fifties, Shirley Abbott left Arkansas more than thirty years ago. She was associated with *Horizon,* the quarterly magazine of the arts, for sixteen years, the last three as editor. But it was her mother's painful death from cancer, plus a national interest in the lives of Southern women, that inspired her to write *Womenfolks*. Abbott believes that she chose to explore her maternal heritage first because "when my mother died in 1968, I was devastated by all kinds of emotions, including regret and guilt. I was horrified by the way she died—of breast cancer. It seemed . . . since she was young, so bitterly unjust to me. And then, when my first child was born in 1970, I missed my mother. I wished I'd had her for a grandmother and a comfort for me.

"There were two things, really, that prompted me to examine my maternal heritage. One was the rise of feminism in which I was keenly interested. Another was my dawning realization that Southern culture was different from other cultures, and it had not been very thoroughly investigated. I think I realized this most clearly when Jimmy Carter was elected and I heard people [in the North] talking about him and about Rosalyn and Miss Lillian and the whole family, and I could see that these people were from Mars" as far as most people were concerned, and "nobody had a clue to what was going on. Of course they were quite familiar to me! I never knew the Carters, but . . . I knew who·these people were; they weren't weird to me at all. Georgia is a different place from Arkansas, but I still thought I understood how they approached things. So I said, 'Well, there really is some room here for somebody to do some explaining.' "

Womenfolks, now a required text on most Women's Studies reading lists, was much more than the story of Abbott's mother, aunts, and grandmothers, whom she traces back to Scotch-Irish peasants who arrived in America in the mideighteenth century. In *Womenfolks*, she also talks about "the Southern identity," the idea that " 'I'm not like you, and though you may send an army against me, I won't give up, and I won't change my ways either, and the reason I won't is that I'm better than you.' This, of course, is the voice of the whipped and defiant, the underdog. Blacks have said the same of themselves against whites. . . . Men of all races, indeed, have used the tactics [of Gandhi and Martin Luther King] against all manner of terrifying antagonists—the church, the law, the military. And women have used it against men. If Southern history has no other meaning, this is the one worth preserving: that there is something better than success, than being top dog, than having the habit of command."

Although Virginia Woolf convinced most writers who are women that we think back through our mothers, after the success of *Womenfolks* Abbott started to wonder about the influence of a father in a daughter's life. "Fathers," she writes in *The Bookmaker's Daughter*, "are supposed to teach their daughters how to be women, that is, how to love and serve them and use them, coexist with them, how to desire them in a seemly manner. A good father domesticates his daughter, so that when she is twenty or so, he can hand her over, polished to a high gloss, to another man. But my father refused to do that. Perhaps he never intended to hand me over to another man. ('Be strong,' he said. 'Depend on no one.')"

But several years had to pass before Abbott was ready to write about Alfred "Hat" Abbott, the "king of the house" on Alamo Street, the charismatic lover of literature who "made book" as the cashier at the notorious Southern Club in Hot Springs and who left for work "on summer mornings . . . in the costume of a gentleman bandit, three-piece ice-cream suit, tailor-made shirt, two-tone shoes, the tiny gold chain across his breast swinging between his pocket watch and his pocket knife, . . . a straw boater shading his eyes. . . . Armed with nothing but a sharp number-two Dixon Ticonderoga pencil, [he] could pay off a three-horse parlay faster than most people could pronounce the names of the horses."

Their father-daughter relationship foundered finally on the issue of integration and on Shirley Abbott's decision to move North. And until recently, she said, "I was not ready to think about my father. In fact, I actively didn't want to think about him. I had buried him, and I was really rather glad to be rid of him. *I mourned him, I don't mean to make myself into a monster of some sort.* But I was glad it was over; I didn't want to think about him; I didn't want to talk about him." Her life with her father, she said, was "gone and forgotten."

However, since the publication of *The Bookmaker's Daughter,* Abbott feels that both books "have been important to me in my personal and psychological development. They have been enormously important in the process of digesting my past and trying to understand myself and my motives. I think, in some way that I probably don't understand yet, becoming a parent motivated me to examine my own heritage. I loved my parents, they did the best they could for me and were wonderful parents in many, many ways, but I was not quite satisfied with my own upbringing. I came out of it bruised in some way, and I came out of it with problems and neuroses and fears that I had to spend a lifetime ridding myself of. And when I had children of my own, I found that I was constantly in an ethical dilemma: What do I do? Do I repeat a pattern, or do I create a new pattern? Am I going to be a trendy mommy, or am I going to stick with the dictates of the past? Or am I going to make some new mix?

"I'm not saying that that experience is unique to me. All educated women go through it, but I think there was something about that process that led me to want to really get down and investigate. I said, 'I'd really like to write about this, which is different than just having it gnaw away at you. You take what's gnawing away at you and you try to make something of it." All of these thoughts "ran together into the same stream, and I guess that had some influence on my chosing first a book about the maternal heritage and then a book about the paternal."

Like many other smart women of her generation (and particularly those from her region of the country), Abbott explained, she had been a child who read her way through childhood. Many of the books—Casanova's memoirs, *Decline and Fall of the Roman Empire, Lorna Doone, The Bride of Lammermoor*—she first encountered behind the glass doors of her father's bookcase in the empty parlor. She says, in fact, that books were "the basis of my father's life. He lived in his head because reality was often so terrible, and he was quite explicit about telling me that reading was the place to live. If you were living in a book, no one could bother you; you could read anywhere. It didn't matter what was going on in your life, and you could have this wonderful life between the covers of a book. I think I knew that from baby-hood, because he said it all the time, in every possible way."

I reminded Abbott that in Josephine Humphreys' novel, *Rich in Love,* the Southern mother complains to the smart Southern daughter: "You live in your head." But Abbott said, "In some cases, it's one's mother who says it. But in my case, it was my father."

The positive effects of this early involvement with reading are obvious: "It turns you into a bookworm. . . . you're bent in an intellectual direction, and perhaps you'll pursue an academic career or a career in writing." But, Abbott believes, there's also the negative effect. "You also get your directions for life from a book. One of the subtexts of *The Bookmaker's Daughter* was that I was kept away from boys until I was at a relatively advanced age, and all I knew about love and about men I picked up from books. I did observe a happy marriage next door, which was very instructive, and an unhappy marriage under my roof, which was also instructive, but when I went out into the world to meet a man of my own, all I knew was what I'd read in romance novels."

Consequently, she says, "it's been a lifelong task to realize that the idea of romance that was marketed to me by all these books is a false idea and a very destructive idea for women in general. So . . . there is a disadvantage to being "a person of the book" when you start that young. . . . You don't want to hear those lessons that come to you from your high school experience, or from your girlfriends' experience, or whatever. I was soaking it all up from these stacks of novels that I was reading. I also got quite a bit of information from the radio—listening to soap operas with my grandmother, and then, of course, movies started feeding in. We listened to 'Just Plain Bill' and 'Ma Perkins' and . . . 'Young Widda Brown,' and 'When a Girl Marries,' and I took that to be a look into the world that was valid and valuable. I took careful notes on what was going on there and figured that I would be dealing with situations like that or, in any case, that that's what life was like. *And I began not to find it too appealing.* When my grandmother said, 'Aren't you going to grow up and get married?' I said, 'No, because all the women on the radio do is cry.' That statement produced great merriment in the household, but it did seem from the information I was getting off the radio that maybe marriage wasn't all it was cracked up to be, whereas, in the books, people were mostly having a good time." At home, on the other hand, and as Abbott writes in *The Book-maker's Daughter,* she "lurched up against the notion that between men and women there is no love, only bargains."

Shirley Abbott says that it is your mother who teaches you "how to deal with men, how to negotiate with them, and how to manage them. And unless you have a brother, the handiest male to try these out on is your father. And either your father allows you to manipulate him and teaches you to be a manipulator, and encourages you to take on this ultrafeminine approach to men, or he doesn't, because you take what you've learned from your mother, and what you've learned from books and learned from watching other women, and you start negotiating with your father. And the most valuable thing my father did for me was that he wouldn't let me manipulate him, and he didn't ask me to manipulate him. He didn't say to me, 'Don't ask me for money until I've had a good meal'; he just said, 'Yes' or 'No.' . . . 'If I've got it, you can have it, and if I don't, you can't. We'll talk about it.' It seemed to me a peer relationship and that I could be honest with him. I didn't need to wrap him around my little finger."

Beyond these specific family stories, what Shirley Abbott has so marvelously accomplished usually falls into the category of memoir. But, she explained, "There are at least two kinds of memoir. One is the kind that a public figure—George Kennan or George Bush or some other George—sits down and writes about where he's been and who he saw, important conferences he attended, and so forth. There is also a form of childhood memoir that is particularized and simply means to set down a record. Those are perfectly fine memoirs, and I have no problem with anybody writing these. But the kind of memoir I write is a different kind of memoir, and there are others who are doing it extremely well." She mentioned as "fine memoirs of the recent past" Vivian Gornick's *Fierce Attachments* and Jill Ker Conway's *The Road from Coorain*.

"I try to get at myself, but I'm not trying to write my story," Abbott says. "I'm trying to examine my past in such a way that it will have value for other people and will help other people examine their own past. I'm trying to do what . . . the *New York Times* reviewer said about Zelda Fitzgerald's writing, that Zelda understood how the arc of the personal life fits into the period or the culture. That's what I hoped to do in these two memoirs." Abbott's plan was to say, "Okay, I'm going to tell you everything I know about myself in this particular arc, and I'm going to do every bit of work I can to connect the personal to the historical and to the political. You come and read this book, and maybe it will be a pathway for you so that you can come along with me, and you can say, 'Oh, yes, that happened to me' or 'That did not happen to me, but something parallel happened to me.' That's what I'm trying to accomplish. I'm not writing for some future biographer, nor do I imagine that my past as a kid in Arkansas was rare and unusual or that someone would want to read it for that reason."

We agreed that to a large extent "all fiction may be autobiography, but all autobiography is of course fiction. I try very hard in this book to describe that process that my father taught me: He always lived by stories. Everything was a narrative. That's why we had dinner: It wasn't to eat; It was so we could tell these stories. And that's why he and I sat on the porch swing together and talked. Because my birth was a story, what happened that day was a story, and I knew darn well that it didn't happen like that. I knew it was different." In fact, she recalled, "my mother used to kind of laugh when she'd hear him spinning these tales for me about what happened on the day I was born. But it was necessary for him; he was the mythmaker in our house, and he made the family myths. My mother made quite a few of her own, and then, when I got the hang of it, I started making some of them myself. That's what we did; we told each other stories all the time. There's that play on words with 'bookmaker' in my book. There's also a play on words with 'stories,' because to my mother, 'to tell a story' meant 'to tell a lie,' and to my father, it meant—'freedom.' "

Shirley Abbott begins *The Bookmaker's Daughter* with an epigraph from *David Copperfield*: "Whether I shall turn out to be the hero of my own life or whether that station will be held by anybody else, these pages must show." She has been singularly successful, having exorcised the demons and illustrated, as only the best writers do, one life.

BOOKS BY SHIRLEY ABBOTT

MEMOIRS

Womenfolks: Growing Up Down South. New York: Ticknor & Fields, 1983; Ticknor & Fields, 1991.

The Bookmaker's Daughter: A Memory Unbound. New York: Ticknor & Fields, 1991.

NONFICTION

The Art of Food. New York: Oxmoor House, 1978.

The National Museum of American History. New York: H. Abrams, 1981.

Charleston. New York: Oxmoor House, 1989.

Jayne Anne Phillips

THE fiction of Jayne Anne Phillips first came to
the attention of the reading public with the publication of *Black Tickets,* a collection of unconven-
tional short stories. *Machine Dreams,* a critically
well-received novel about the effects of the Vietnam War on a Bellington, West Virginia, family,
followed. Her second collection of stories, *Fast
Lanes,* was published in 1987, its tone established by a character in the title story who says,
"Don't drive in the fast lane unless you're pass-

ing." "Why not?" replies the narrator. "I pass everything anyway, so I might as well stay in the fast lane. I like fast lanes!"

Unlike many of her rootless characters, Jayne Anne Phillips, now the consummate suburbanite, lives in a multiroomed, wood-paneled house in Newton, Massachusetts, complete with a verandah and framed by six sprawling chestnut trees whose gnarled branches are twisted into an umbrella of green leaves. We talked over Thai food in a nearby village restaurant, between childcare responsibilities for her two young sons, Soren (after Kierkegaard and several characters in Chekhov's plays) and the tow-haired Theo. Although Phillips is now immersed in what she calls the "young child stage of life," she continues to work "on a novel that seems to be taking forever."

"I started out as a poet and became a short-story writer, and I spent several years writing stories, but writing *Machine Dreams* spoiled me for short stories," she said. "I remember when I was writing poems and I discovered paragraphs, . . . I stopped writing broken lines and went on from there to writing prose poems and very, very compressed fiction, and from there to writing a novel. And now I find that I really think in novels; I don't think of things in terms of short stories anymore.

"I remember how free I felt when I stopped writing poems, although writing in paragraphs always seemed to me to be very subversive, and the novel seems even more subversive than the short story. You can be reading the newspaper or the directions on how to put together a tent, . . . but the writer's voice in the paragraph form sinks into the reader's consciousness without the reader defending against it. When you are reading a poem," on the other hand, "you're always aware that you are reading a poem, because of the way it looks on the page."

Perhaps, she suggested, the reason she now prefers writing novels is "that you live with a novel for so many years that you begin to have a relationship with it the way you would have with a person. With the short story you do have more of a sense of control. I know what Alice Munro means when she speaks about a thread moving through it. With the novel, you don't have that sense of control at all, at least until you're almost finished, because the novel itself is a kind of mystery that the characters are moving around in." How form affects fiction, she added, is "a strange thing. It has to do with the relationship each writer has to the process."

Although Phillips's reputation was established with her short stories, she remains aware, as are most writers of both short stories and novels, that the reading public tends to value the novelist more. As Francine Prose has remarked, nobody ever says, "Working on another short story?" But Phillips thinks that "maybe what people respect more, or have more misunderstanding about, is the idea that when you're writing you're sort of adrift in a boat, kind of out there somewhere. . . . Writing a novel does take five years, four years, three years, eight years; you're out there a long time. And sometimes you come back with a good book, and sometimes you don't, but you're out there regardless. And maybe that's what people respect or feel some awe about.

"I'm interested in writing about the way people perceive things, the way memory works, the way that memory has a kind of natural selection that picks out the most important things. But I think the reason I've been interested in writing about the family is that it's a kind of microcosm of the whole world."

I suggested that in *Machine Dreams* the memories on which this family depends do not keep it rooted; the characters seemed particularly estranged and alienated from each other. Peter Nelson was correct when he wrote in *VIS à VIS* magazine, "There is a sense of intrusion in [Phillips's] work, obligation intruding on solitude, death intruding on life, chaos ever seeping through the cracks. . . . Her characters strive mightily to protect themselves, though usually they can't. They are hard and smart and heroic and they suffer anyway."

But Phillips says: "What I'm writing about is just reality. Regardless of whether there is a divorce or a death in the family, every family falls apart because the children grow up, the parents die, and they stop living together. Everybody has that experience of first loss, which is just the fact that people grow up. Most children, for some short period of time, have that sense of being wrapped within the family; it may be a dysfunctional family, but there still is that incredible structure that, to children in particular, seems everlasting. And I think when I write about these bonds breaking up, I'm not even so much talking about rootlessness, or what's happening in America, or the good old days versus the bad old days, or the past versus the present. I'm just talking about . . . the way things come to an end, the way everything comes to an end, and the way . . . human beings deal with loss, move beyond it, are either buried by it or stand on top of it and go on to something else.

"If people live long enough, the child becomes the parent and that is an inversion, and if we are lucky enough to live natural, long lives, everyone goes through that; it's part of the process." Phillips is, in fact, annoyed by the reviewers who say, "My world is about a family falling apart. My sense of it is that I am just talking about reality; the family does fall apart. And it's meant to, in fact. The children are meant to grow up and move away and live their lives, and that's the fascinating thing about family.

"The thing that's interesting about the 1990s as compared with the 1930s and the 1940s," Phillips says, "is that people no longer have stereotypical relationships; they no longer have certain narrow boundaries to define what father and mother is; there are so many different kinds of families now, so many children growing up with one parent in one house and another parent in the other, or families that are not made up of married people or blood-related people. In a way, people have to be even more responsible about defining their relationships because they can't lean on those old definitions. Everything has to be reexamined and recognized. . . . I think the writer, too, is always trying to redeem something. Even if you are writing about the most dysfunctional family in the world, if you write a book in which these people come alive and a period of time that is alive (and yet frozen within the book), you've saved it because you've encapsulated it. The book may not be the actual history of that family, but you have redeemed some spiritual version of it."

These remarks are in part applicable to Phillips's own life, since she is far from her hometown in West Virginia, where "you have to drive sixty miles to get a copy of the *New York Times Book Review* and, of course, no one does that," and they raise the obvious questions about biography as material for fiction and the less obvious question of how a writer's work is affected by where she currently lives. Phillips thinks that the effect of place "probably depends on what you're writing. Right now I think the place where I live is functioning as a protection, a kind of asbestos covering. I don't think I would be able to write about my childhood, or something that draws on my childhood, if I hadn't left that place and gone far away."

And it is clear that Jayne Anne Phillips wants that protection because she sees herself as an isolated person. "I always felt isolated. I might have been isolated, regardless of where I grew up. After all, there are many people who grew up in West Virginia who weren't like me at all. It's probably more a function of your primal family. I was the typical writer in the family, the one responsible for the family stories and the family myths, the one who listened to it all. The others couldn't have cared less. In my case, it happened because I was a girl; if there had been another daughter, I might have been a biologist.

"In that place, the women were responsible for all of that emotional terrain. So when I write in a direct way, I just naturally write about West Virginia because my growing-up years were anchored there. It is useful because it was such a removed place, such an isolated place, and it works well for my work. . . . To me, being isolated is being protected. Even if writers seem to be outgoing, there is always a core of real aloneness. I think you almost have to have that to write."

Phillips will need this isolation for the book she plans to undertake after the current novel is completed, when "my kids are a little older. It's going to be a difficult book to write, and I will need a certain amount of silence around me." The book will deal with the death of her mother from lung cancer. "I think in my mother's case it might have been radon, the invisible gas that is in all our houses. (You're supposed to have your house tested for it.) That's all I can figure out. She did smoke for twenty years, but she only smoked about a pack a week and she quit twenty years ago—completely. She hadn't had a cigarette in twenty years and all of a sudden she turns up with lung cancer, so I don't know."

Unfortunately, Phillips's grandmother also died of cancer, and Phillips's mother "engineered her mother's death at a very young age." By "engineered" she means that her mother was responsible for her grandmother, a part of the story she has written about in her work "in other ways." Phillips's mother "was the last child living at home, living with her mother who was sick with cancer. Her mother died at home and my mother, at twenty-two or twenty-three, took care of her. In the last few weeks there was a family friend, who was also a nurse, who moved in, and they did [the caregiving] together. My mother had no children at the time, she was living in her mother's space, and it was different from what happened later to me." But the fact is that when Phillips's mother died, "it was death by cancer, with a daughter caring for her mother, and it was a repeat of history. And, in a way, this business of taking care of my mother was something I was prepared to do all my life—because I'd heard all of these stories of how my mother had cared for her mother and done it perfectly.

"Although I don't think much about my role as a daughter any more (I guess I consider myself an orphan), I was greatly identified with my mother. She was alone, and when she died I felt as though I had lost her completely because the illness was so debilitating, and the relationship was so strained, and she was not herself. . . . I was the mother (she would even call me 'Mother'), but I wasn't able to save her, as a mother should save a child. . . . I knew that I wasn't able to save her, but when she got to the point when she wasn't thinking clearly, it wasn't clear to her that I couldn't. I've read a lot of books about dying and the process of dying. Often the chief caregiver is the one blamed:

All the fears are foisted off on that person, and that was, in part, what happened. I was an adult looking at it, but I was also her child looking at it, and her disappointment in me and her disapproval of me, as a child, was also there, mixed up in it all. I'm left with a feeling that I failed her in some way. And through that failure, I feel as though I didn't just lose her, I also lost the relationship itself, as a memory or as a support."

With the history of cancer in her family, Phillips knows it "would make perfect sense for me to face the same situation. But, on the other hand, I'm a terrible driver; I drive fast. And I don't pay that much attention. And all of that I have to use in a future novel."

Although most writers are reluctant to talk about work in progress, Phillips says that her current book is "about girl children, but I took it out of the family context because I wanted to see it away from mothers. It really is about unmothered daughters, about girls on their own, faced with a kind of almost devil incarnate. When I see evil as a symbology, it somehow has to do with myself and my mother, the evil that sort of inhabited her, because that is what happens. The person is in there somewhere, but imprisoned in this transforming physical self."

Phillips and I, who were both feeling pressured by deadlines and responsibilities that day, talked about time, the precious commodity that writers crave, and the frequent suggestion that women write at the expense of their children. On this subject Phillips said, "There is some trouble from other people, but my experience is that the writer has more trouble from herself. I have felt a lot of pressure that the kids are my first responsibility, and I can't do anything else until they are taken care of. My schedule is totally at the mercy of their schedule. If one of them is sick, I don't work that day. If there is a school vacation, I don't work that day. And, what's even worse, if the au pair quits, I don't work that day [or ever again] until I can find a new one. As a profession writing is totally dependent on your child-care situation, and it's very, very frustrating. I refer to it as the 'au pair wars.' Everywhere I go (and this is not just for people in the arts), women who are trying to do any kind of work have to deal with day-care centers or nannies or au pairs or live-in students or something."

In spite of this, Jayne Anne Phillips continues to teach, usually at Brandeis University. "If I say anything to students," she said, "It's write what you are compelled to write. I don't deal with what you know or what you don't know. I think the real energy comes from our obsessions and our compulsions, and what we are obsessed with is a real clue to what we want to write about. . . . When you have already created the world of your book, and you are in the spirit of it, maybe you go look at pictures of cars that existed at that time, or you listen to the music that was played then on popular radio stations, and you immerse yourself in certain things about the world. You sink deeper into the feeling of living in that era. But the story line arises from obsession with the material, and I don't think you know the story line; you write the book to find out what the story is. In fact, that is what the writer learns from writing, and it is probably the reason the writer writes."

The problem with teaching writing, at least for Jayne Anne Phillips, is that "my boundaries are not well-defined, and when I teach I get emotionally involved. What seems to happen is that people in the class deal with whatever is most pressing to them, and I end up reading their stories at night in bed when I'm practically unconscious. I start out by having them write autobiography; I talk about selective memory, the transformation of what really happened, and from the beginning, especially with younger students, I talk about taking risks. I try to prove to them that there's nothing you can't write about, and usually there's a lot of intense stuff that people start dealing with. That's what I find so involving: so much energy going on between people. I can edit something without thinking too hard about it, but you're not just editing; you're really dealing with people's lives. . . . Hopefully, what happens is that they learn to step back [from their own experience] to save themselves."

Phillips also verbalized what many writers believe: "Writers are writers by the time they are about seven. Whether they go on to write is an accident of how their lives turn out." She believes also that "the writer is essentially an outsider, and any artist tries to live beyond the limits of his or her own personality. You are not just yourself; you have access to an entirely different dimension. I don't mean to sound Twilight Zone-ish, because that's not what I mean. But the surprise that's within painting or composing or writing is the idea that it can go somewhere that you don't know about, that you can't expect, that you can't control, that you don't want to control (because, in fact, you can go further if you don't control it, and if you just follow it). The compulsion to write comes from knowing that [this phenomenon] can happen. It doesn't always happen, but you have access to it . . . and watching it happen is part of being a writer.

"I think," she said, "that we keep writing and we keep trying because art is what is going to move us beyond . . . ourselves. It allows us to find out what kind of people we are, and what kind of people we could be. In my first book there was a line, instead of a disclaimer: 'Love or loss lends a reality to what is imagined.' I think that is true and that is what writers are dealing with."

BOOKS BY JAYNE ANNE PHILLIPS

NOVELS

Machine Dreams. New York: E. P. Dutton / Seymour Lawrence, 1984; Pocket Books, 1985.

SHORT STORIES

Sweethearts. Short Beach, Ct.: Truck Press, 1976. (Limited edition)
Counting. New York: Vehicle Editions, 1978. (Limited edition)
Black Tickets. New York: Delacorte Press, 1979; Delta, 1979.

How Mickey Made It. St. Paul: Bookslinger Press, 1981.
(Limited edition)
The Secret Country. Winston-Salem, N.C.: Palaemon, 1982.
(Limited edition)
Fast Lanes. New York: E. P. Dutton / Seymour Lawrence, 1987;
Washington Square Press, 1988.

Sue Miller

SUE MILLER'S husband, the novelist Douglas Bauer, writes in an office at their home in Boston's South End. And since she is very protective of his privacy, we agreed to meet at one of the noisy cappuccino bars on Newberry Street that are wedged between the consumer palaces of Fendi and Gucci, where recession-proof Bostonians shop.

Miller—whose first novel, *The Good Mother*, stayed on the *New York Times* bestseller list for twenty-four weeks and was probably the most discussed novel of 1986—arrived on that cold Massachusetts day dressed in a purple sweater, black slacks, a serviceable suede coat, and light brown, lace-up granny boots. Sue Miller was on her way to her office at Boston University to finish grading final exams so that she could leave town for several months to work on her latest novel.

Although it is hard not to think of this writer as a superstar (when you know that paperback rights for *The Good Mother* were auctioned for $840,000 and the first printing was 1.4 million copies), you are immediately struck by her modest dress and demeanor. But that should not be confused with her forthrightness. After several hours of conversation, this interviewer was thoroughly disabused of her own cherished beliefs about women who write: One, that they are not comfortable "talking money," and two, that most women writers do not usually comment, for publication, on their own reviews or on the films that are made from their novels. Sue Miller does both.

The Good Mother is the story of a divorced woman, Anna Dunlop (whose first name purposely evokes Anna Karenina), and the custody fight for her young daughter, Molly. The legal debacle results from Anna's passionate involvement with Leo, an artist. When Brian (Anna's ex-husband) sues to regain custody of Molly, alleging that Leo is guilty of "sexual irregularities" with his child, a caseworker discovers that Anna and Leo once made love while Molly was asleep in bed with them. On another occasion, while he was in the shower, Leo "responded sexually" when Molly innocently touched him. As Josephine Humphreys wrote in *The Nation,* the issue becomes "whether a woman can lose her child if the man she loves makes a mistake, and how hard she will fight to defend him," since "Anna is sure of Leo's innocence, or at least of the innocence of his intent." By the novel's end, Anna understands that she is living a nightmare, having somehow succumbed to what she calls a "euphoric forgetfulness of all the rules," something a "good mother" must never do. The novel spotlights in various ways what the book jacket, and the tide of publicity, called "the conflict . . . between two powerful sets of feelings, the erotic and the maternal."

The Good Mother was made into a disappointing movie starring Diane Keaton and directed by Leonard Nimoy, of Mr. Spock fame. Of course, I wanted to know what Miller thought of it and what her role was in the production of the film. Interestingly, she had no involvement at all, and she said that the "issue in selling *The Good Mother* to the movies was money exclusively." Miller reminded me that she took the advice attributed to Ernest Hemingway: " 'You take the book to the California state line, you throw it over, they throw you the money, then you go back to where you came from,' and that's really the way I felt about it. You know," she continued, "the story of the writer in Hollywood has been done, and it's apparent to anyone who has read about it that you are really just nobody out there." Miller also revealed that she had not seen the movie of *The Good Mother*. "If they want to buy [subsequent novels], I'll take the money again, if they offer it to me, because it buys me, and it buys my husband, time to write.

"People talk about the movie version of a book, but I don't think there is a movie version of any book—it's just a movie. The movie people were very kind and very gracious to me, and they were willing to listen to any input I might have, but I feel as though I'm a writer and . . . that wasn't my job. I didn't want to learn how to do any of that or learn how to think that way, and I didn't want to see the movie. I wanted to think of *The Good Mother* exactly as I had always thought of it and not have some sudden visual image from somewhere else. . . . I actually thought it might be damaging psychologically to see it."

Miller thinks a writer would be naive to imagine she would have significant control over the process of transformation from novel into film. "That process is so incredibly different, and the history of films made from books is by and large a pretty sorry one. I think any writer does well to note that at the start and to just make a decision: Do you want the money? Do you feel disassociated enough from the film to do that without being distressed in some way?"

The fact that this particular novel, which seems to have been read by nearly every woman in America, was directed by a man also was of little concern to Miller. "I think that most of the women directors are independent filmmakers, and there aren't a lot who are employed by big-buck producers or by studios, . . . and none of *them* had expressed any interest." But it was "clear when [Touchstone Films, the adult arm of Walt Disney Productions,] first bought the book who the director was going to be." And, in any case, "everything is collaborative in the film world, and it's all for the sake of profit. There's a whole different approach; the process itself is collaborative." Miller says, in fact, that she doesn't even know her Hollywood agent. "I met him once when I was doing a reading out there, and he came up and introduced himself. But our relationship is all business." Overall, Miller stressed the positive, however. "Producers are so desperate for something with a plot that they are buying books at an incredible rate. It seems to me a wonderful opportunity for writers."

Sue Miller is similarly philosophical about the sale, this time to television, of her second best-selling novel, *Family Pictures,* which took four years to complete. "I naturally have an aversion to television since these people sit down and do deals and negotiate with each other endlessly—have lunch and package and that sort of thing, . . . but, finally, I thought, what's the difference? It's going to be something I don't feel connected to, . . . and there wasn't any real bidding for the movie rights. It would have taken someone incredibly committed to the book, with a very particular vision, to see a movie in *Family Pictures.* The book is much less plot driven, it doesn't cry out for a visual version the way *The Good Mother* did."

Family Pictures deals with a suburban Chicago family, one of whose six children, Randall, is an autistic boy. As Laura Shapiro wrote in *Newsweek,* it is "a novel steeped in the details of home and family life, but [it uses] those details to gain access to wider, deeper truths." Randall's presence changes everything in David and Lainey's marriage and reverberates in the household like his cries at night. According to the experts of the fifties, the fault is Lainey's for unconsciously rejecting her infant son; David—himself a psychiatrist—agrees with them." It is a novel about betrayal on many levels.

I wondered whether Miller was concerned that Randall might be portrayed in a monstrous way, in spite of the sympathetic handling of autism in such films as *Rainman,* with Dustin Hoffman. "I trust not," said Miller, "but I don't know. While we were in negotiation, I wrote the producer that I would prefer [that Randall's condition in *Family Pictures*] not be turned into the disease of the week. I think that they want to focus . . . on the different members of the family, to look at it more as a family drama. But it's really their business."

Miller also mentions the practical advantage of having her novels appear as movies or TV dramas. "People might read the book as a result of seeing the television drama, and I'm grateful to have new readers. Anything that will broaden the audience for serious fiction is good. I had very nice letters from people who read *The Good Mother* in paperback after having seen the movie, and they said with great surprise that they liked the book better, and they couldn't say why. [I] remember having an argument with my son, who, in the young, kneejerk kind of way," had his own problems with the paperback: " 'Ma, how could you do this?' " he told Miller. " 'It's going to be in airports!' " She said, "Why be such a snot? Why shouldn't I want as many people to read it as possibly can? Don't you believe in literature? Don't you believe that it can touch or move anyone? I am delighted that it has a glitzy cover and an airport rack and that it is available to people who are enjoying it." She said that if a movie treatment, paperback, or television version increases her readership, "It's wonderful. . . . If it does that; who can object? I'm pleased," she said emphatically, "to have that happen."

In that sense, Miller says, "I am very interested in the reader of the book, in touching people, and less interested in . . . experiments with language. I am careful about such things, but I don't think that is my particular gift; I'm a storyteller in an unfashionable way, and that's my interest. That's the kind of book I always like to read, one that offers me an alternative universe to inhabit for a while."

Miller particularly likes the work of Joan Chase and Alice Munro. "I love Alice Munro—she is a real genius—and I love *That Night* by Alice McDermott. These writers are really interested in stories and in lives. One of the things I tried to master in *The Good Mother* was the notion of a plot. And sure enough I did, and I think in part that was what made the book so commercially viable. It was very much a story, and I very much wanted the story to be dramatic."

In *Family Pictures,* on the other hand, "there were other things I wanted to master. In some sense I was turning away from plot and wanted to move, in the third person, among a whole group of characters. I'd felt rather enclosed by the first-person perspective of *The Good Mother*. By the end of that book I was itching to be working with multiple perspectives. So when I was thinking of what to do next, I struggled with trying not to repeat a certain kind of success. Later, I sent a bit of the manuscript to a friend who had been an editor, and she wrote back and said, 'Well, this is certainly not *The Good Mother*,' and I felt very relieved. I didn't want to repeat *The Good Mother,* but I didn't want to be trapped into doing something purely in defiance of the success of *The Good Mother;* I didn't want to be trapped that way either."

Miller grew up on the street where *Family Pictures* is set, near the University of Chicago. "Although I wanted to use my own childhood, where in some way I would feel involved and held by memory, we were a family of four without a problem, without an issue, not in the way that this family has." Certainly, she says, we "looked much more normal from the outside and our process through life was much less overtly rebellious." It was a "certain universe" that she left early because she "went away to college [B. A., Radcliffe, 1964] at sixteen. My parents moved while I was away at college, so there really wasn't a place to come back to, and I never lived at home after that, except in the summertime."

Sue Miller seems concerned that critics understand what she is trying to accomplish in her books. She feels there has been a "lack of metaphoric discussion of *The Good Mother* and of *Family Pictures* too. Women's writing generally is discussed, very concretely, as if . . . it were written for women exclusively and as though the lives of female characters couldn't be metaphors for life in general. Social issues that affect women's lives are always discussed, as though the novel were really written as a kind of essay with a plot attached." Miller also comments about "the failure of feminist reviewers and literary critics to see beyond the feminist issues" in novels. "In a certain sense, women who write fiction and political feminists come from two different camps. One is interested in change and revolution; the other, women who write serious fiction, believes that life doesn't change that much, that we all struggle perennially with the same old painful issues that are true for all people: how to deal with unexplained suffering, how to survive a sorrowful universe, how to heal yourself, how to restore yourself when that seems difficult and impossible (given what life deals out to people). That's not a very revolutionary approach to take—to speak of sorrow and suffering as inevitable and as part of the human condition. And yet all serious writers have always spoken that way." The problem is that this concept is "politically unthinkable for a deeply passionate feminist in some way or another."

Miller objects to "the critical discussion of women writers as women, rather than as literary people concerned with painful, truthful images. That discussion has tended to isolate critical discussion of women's fiction, has tended to make women's fiction seem more directed to women than to men. In order for women to be successful, men need to be reading their work and seeing it as having metaphorical possibilities for them! They need to see that the reality of midtwentieth-century female life can be metaphorically as true as the life of a whaling captain with all the technological information about that life. In that case, the details are all metaphor, and they are all metaphor in the case of a woman writer too." The "metaphor of home and of making a home and family is as powerful for both genders as the idea of hitting the road or chasing after white whales ever was."

Miller admits that she "felt singularly called to task by the feminist reviewing community for *The Good Mother*: The heroine wasn't heroic enough, she was a fool in her response to the psychiatrist [who examines her during the custody proceedings], . . . all these things, which may or may not be true, who knows? But on the other hand, I don't know many people who are heroic in that way." Actually, "that was not even what I was getting at. I was talking about someone into whose life a terrible thing was thrust—partly because of her own foolishness, but with her highest hopes too. And I felt that I was writing a character's life that could stand in for anyone's life.

"The truly feminist act, as I see it, is to imagine that your character has a universal value, metaphorically speaking, and to feel that and to write that way. I think that one feels most trapped as a woman by the kind of criticism that says, 'She is telling us that women can do this, that women must do this and mustn't do this,' and the reality, I suspect, is that most women who write aren't telling women a goddamn thing. They are trying to tell everybody something about where one finds the nerve to get on with it, to go on with it, or doesn't. But I cannot be ungrateful for the attention *[The Good Mother]* got and for the serious discussion that it had."

Miller goes on to say that with *Family Pictures* "it's been interesting to me that the mother and daughter . . .—and the mother particularly—are the characters reviewers picked up on again. Whereas I thought I was working with a much larger range of characters and with issues that had to do with father / son problems and male sexuality too. . . . There is a very narrow way of looking at women's work; it's as if the rest of that book didn't exist."

I suggested that what should have been discussed more was the issue of silence. Miller seemed to agree. "I certainly meant Randall's silence to work in the novel in a quite specific way. He would be very mysterious, and very blank, and therefore open the way for different versions" of family myths. "Most families (most of the time) don't agree on their myths and [the existence of] Randall is an extreme example of a destructive factor who suddenly fractures the idea of the unified myth. Often in families there are these mysterious arguments about whose fault the fracture is. I mean, 'It really was Mom,' or 'Dad was such a jerk,' or 'Who was wrong?' but in this case there is no question. What it *means* is up for grabs. We make our own picture of [reality] and to the degree that we're open to other people's versions, we can change that picture. But I'm struck with how absolute an image can be, and how unchangeable it is over time."

Miller was herself raised in a big family. "It always seems to me that it's a gift if you listen to the other person's version of the family myths and then correct yours in some way. I worry about someone like my son [now twenty-three] who grew up as an only child. He really doesn't have all these other versions of the family myth which can be beneficial, at least in terms of personal growth."

Sue Miller is singularly self-contained, thoughtful, and introspective. She is both forthcoming in her responses to questions and, at the same time, removed and graciously self-protective. About her personal life she is willing to say that she is now happily married. When she was much younger she "married someone who came back to Boston to go through a residency; then we were divorced and I just stayed. At the time my child was two, two and a half, and I had a group of friends whom one could count on for help. And once you stay for a while, then your child also gets connected to his group, and so through inertia, through ease and comfort, here I am. I stayed on forever." But one should not assume that Boston has now become the so-called right place for Sue Miller. In fact, Miller said, "I don't feel at home anywhere, and I think that may help me in some ways. I don't feel at home in Chicago either, although I sort of . . . yearn for the home that was there. It was a place where I did feel at home until I left. I was very young, and a lot of the withdrawal for me, the onedayness of writing *Family Pic-*

tures, was dwelling on that place again for awhile." This particular brand of homesickness does not seem to be related to the sense of exile or separateness that many writers feel. "It's specific to me," Sue Miller says. "I'm just an uncomfortable person, and a very anxious person" who is happiest with her husband and few close friends.

But, she said with a gracious smile, like most good writers she is writing "that sort of universal story of how you make your way around the dragon, or how you slay the dragon, or how the dragon slays you," and there is, she remembered, "that wonderful line from Chekhov: 'I must believe in progress because it was so much better after they stopped beating me than while they were beating me.' I believe," said Sue Miller, "that some things can get better, but I also believe in human sorrow."

BOOKS BY SUE MILLER

NOVELS

The Good Mother. New York: Harper & Row, 1986; Dell, 1987.
Family Pictures. New York: Harper & Row, 1990; Harper Paperbacks, 1991.

SHORT STORIES

Inventing the Abbotts. New York: Harper & Row, 1987; Dell, 1988.

Lois Lowry

ALTHOUGH the fictional, brown-haired, and bespectacled teenager named Anastasia Krupnick has long since moved from a Cambridge apartment to a Victorian house in the suburbs, her creator, Lois Lowry, still lives in a red-brick condominium, with a geranium-filled terrace, on Boston's Beacon Hill. Her cozy studio, filled with patchwork quilts and wicker furniture, is tucked away in a historic coachhouse off a terraced courtyard garden a few blocks away.

Lois Lowry is one of America's most successful authors of books for children and young adults. The Krupnick family— Anastasia (now thirteen) and her younger brother Sam (a certified genius), her mother Katherine Klein, an illustrator who works at home, and her father, Myron, a professor of poetry at Harvard—appears in nine novels to date. And, as Lowry says, there will be more books in this series because "I think my psyche requires amusement from time to time, and the Anastasia books provide that. They are very easy to write because I know all the characters, I know where the books are set, I know where Anastasia lives, and I know her friends. And, while I try to introduce new elements in each book, the basic stuff is all there. So when I just need to relax and tee-hee a little to myself, I say, 'It's time to write another book about Anastasia.' The publisher, of course, is delighted, because the books have a built-in audience; the publisher doesn't have to go out and create one."

Lois Lowry has also brought to her young readers (and to many of their parents) a discussion of life's harsher realities. *Autumn Street,* her favorite book, deals with the death of a young boy. In *Find a Stranger, Say Goodbye,* Natalie, who is named for her eccentric grandmother, Hallie, searches for her birth mother. The character of Hallie was patterned after a male artist who lived on Cranberry Island, off the coast of Maine, whom Lowry photographed for a magazine. *Us and Uncle Fraud,* the story of a visit by the black sheep of an extremely conventional family, deals with expectation, disappointment, disaster, and the power of love. (Since Lowry is a football fan, the young boy in the novel is named Marcus, after her "favorite football player.") Her first book, *A Summer to Die* (set in Lowry's 150-year-old farmhouse in New Hampshire, which she uses on weekends), grew from the story of her own sister, who, like Molly Chalmers in this novel, died very young. "In the summertime, there are masses of yellow flowers in front of the windows, flowers called Helenium, which means 'Helen's flower.' I planted them in memory of her, and I wrote the book for the same reason."

Although her books are enriched by a sense of resolution and contentment, Lois Lowry has had more than a passing acquaintance with pain. In reality, her life, like our conversation during the interview, has taken a circuitous route.

"I got married when I was nineteen, and I was married for twenty-one years. When my husband graduated from Brown University, I'd just finished my sophomore year, but he wanted to get married, and, in those days, that's what women did. So there I was, married and just turned nineteen, and by the time I was twenty-five I had four children, all under the age of four. My husband was a lawyer, and I was a housewife in Maine with four babies, which was not his fault. I'd chosen that! I loved having those babies; I don't regret it. When my kids started school, I went back and got my college degree (it took me four years to finish the two years that I needed) and went to graduate school. And I'm sure I got a lot more out of college in my thirties than when I was eighteen and worrying about clothes and dates. By now you can perceive [in this story] that I'm getting pretty old. After that I began writing professionally. I was working as a freelance journalist, but also being supported in the manner to which I had become accustomed as a wife of a lawyer. I didn't have to live on that journalist's income, so it was a comfy, neat way to make a living. I quit the Junior League and all that stuff, and I had this little career carved out."

Lowry wrote her "first book for kids about the time of my fortieth birthday. The book was published the same spring my husband and I split up. I sometimes have said, 'There is no cause and effect there,' but that's not true, because what was happening, as I look at it in retrospect, is that I wasn't that person he'd married anymore. And he didn't want to be married to somebody who now said she was a writer and was going to go off and do stuff and earn money."

Lowry recalled an experience "from those late years of my marriage, when I was beginning to take my own writing seriously. We lived in a house with walls of bookcases and a room with a big antique rolltop desk. That was *his* desk. Not that my husband ever did any work at home. He had an office that he went to every day, but a lawyer had to have a study at home. So when I started writing seriously, I had a small table put in the corner of the study and I put my electric typewriter there, which my *father* bought for me, and that's where I did my thing. Looking back, I picture myself as a little mouse sitting in the corner of a room in which everything belonged to someone else, except that corner. One thing I do feel angry about, and that was when I went away to do some magazine work and came back during the day. The kids were in school, my husband was at the office, and I came in and dropped my suitcase, looked around—and my typewriter was gone. I panicked. I called my husband at the office and said, 'The house has been broken into, and they've stolen my typewriter!' And he said, "No, nobody has stolen your typewriter. He had *loaned* it to somebody while I was gone! Well, I see you rolling your eyes. He didn't perceive, and I think still wouldn't perceive, what a dagger to my heart that was. He loaned my typewriter to somebody; it's as if I loaned his balls to somebody. . . . So he married somebody else and I didn't."

Lowry understands the ways in which early experiences influence more recent actions, and we talked about some of them. For instance, Lowry says that she has used an agent "for the last three books, but it's not to sell books. I think I've written nineteen, and the same publisher has published all of them, so I didn't need an agent for that. I needed an agent to deal with the money part, not because it comes in huge amounts, but because I've had the same editor for all those books. He and I have become good friends over the years, and I, being a (female) product of my generation, don't feel comfortable asking my good friend for money. So I have an agent to deal with that tangential business stuff. I was married to a man who did all that, and I just never had to deal with the marketplace. And, of course, I chose a profession, a very solitary, introverted profession (not that I chose it, I think it was always a part of me), and I never cast about for another which would have me out there dealing with confrontational issues."

She recounted how her anxieties are dramatically reflected in her dreams, especially in a recurring dream that seems to relate both to her personal and professional life. "I dream that I have a baby and I am not taking care of it and I have forgotten about it: I have forgotten to name it, I've forgotten to buy clothes for it, and I haven't fed it in a long time. And in my dream I rush, panic-stricken, to the crib or the carriage where this baby is. It's a great relief because it's not only okay, it's better than every other baby. . . . It has a full set of teeth, . . . and the baby says, 'Hey, I'm okay.' And that always happens when I'm working on a book and not paying enough attention to it. And if the baby is over there [gesturing in the direction of the studio], and I'm not taking care of it, I have this dream. Sometimes the dream doesn't end happily; sometimes I drop the baby and it breaks. But sometimes, after the book is finished, I put the baby on a boat, sort of a ferry boat, and wave."

While the "baby" in this dream is most obviously a book, or Lowry's own talent, she relates it to other things. "When I was divorced, the younger kids were fourteen and fifteen, and the other two were in college. But there were times when I've been very concerned about my kids and about whether I was taking care of them. They are all okay except for the problems that one can't do anything about. One of my daughters is very ill, and the illness is not curable, and I am devastated over this tragedy."

The unattended-baby dream is somewhat mitigated by "a recurrent, very good dream. I wake up and I'm so happy I had this dream. I'm living in a house, not a house in which I've actually lived, and I suddenly discover a door or stairway that I haven't known was there, and there are all these rooms that I didn't know I had, and they are fabulous! It's hard to get to them because you have to climb up this stairway, but then there are these terrific rooms!" Anyone who has ever tried to create anything—whether it's a book or a recipe for spaghetti sauce—can identify with this dream.

Lois Lowry is also an acute observer of the not-always-understandable experiences that are lost on more literal people, but are fictional fuel for writers. "There's a particular space I always have in my mind, a room, and there's always a window and a rug in the corner. A number of years ago I was walking past a graphic arts gallery on Newberry Street in Boston, and I went in because it was so cold outside. There were six serigraphs on exhibit, and I stopped short because . . . they were pictures of this space that I have in my head. One of them was saying, 'Buy me.' " said Lowry, and even though "they were expensive, seven hundred dollars apiece," she was tempted. When she asked the salesman "if the little sticker on it meant that it was sold," he said, " 'The oddest thing happened yesterday. . . . Someone came in here and stood like you did and said, "I have to have that picture. I didn't come here to buy anything, but that serigraph is a picture of my dream." ' "

A similar story reveals another way in which Lowry makes connections to people who feel a natural sympathy with her. "I am," she said, "not knowledgeable about astrology, nor do I have a strong opinion about it one way or another. But I have had an experience that I find interesting and disconcerting. . . . I've traveled a great deal over the years, doing conferences and making speeches, so I'm constantly smiling at new people whom I will never see again, . . . but every now and then I'll meet somebody with whom I have some point of contact and with whom I remain friends. And, in a startlingly large number of instances, these people turn out to have my same birthday, March twentieth. My publisher sent me to Australia a few years back, and I had to speak in five different cities. Before I left, I got a letter from a writer named Diane Burns who said she admired my work. She hoped we would meet, but the distances were so great and I wasn't going to be in her city, so it was unlikely. However, she wanted to welcome me to Australia.

"When I left for Australia I took with me a big shopping bag full of T-shirts that said 'Boston' (with a picture of the skyline across the front), and every now and then, at speaking engagements, I'd give away a shirt at an Anastasia lookalike contest. There are always little girls with glasses, and many of them look like Anastasia, or so I thought.

"Then one time I was in a town on the coast near Sydney. I looked out into the audience and saw that none of the kids was wearing glasses. I thought, 'Well, how can I give away this shirt?' . . . Years ago I'd read someplace that in any group of fifty, the chances are that two people will have the same birthday as you. So I figured I'd try that. If anybody had my same birthday, they'd get the T-shirt. I tantalized them a bit . . . and finally revealed that the month was March, and then I worked my way through the days until I said it was the twentieth. Their mouths fell open. No one had my birthday. But then in the back of the room, this woman stood up and said, 'My birthday's March twentieth,' . . . and it was Diane Burns."

The epiphanic event also surfaces in Lowry's recent novel, *Number the Stars,* which deals with a Christian family's rescue of their Jewish neighbors, the Rosens, during the Nazi occupation of Denmark. Through the eyes of ten-year-old Annemarie Johansen, Lowry describes how members of the Danish Resistance managed to smuggle almost the entire Jewish population, nearly 7,000 people, across the sea to Sweden. Lowry, herself a Norwegian-American, flew to Copenhagen to reexperience the city she had visited many years before. "I thought I could write the book without going to Denmark, and in fact I'd written a good part of it when I suddenly had the feeling that I needed to go back there. . . . Since I don't speak Danish (nobody speaks Danish except the Danes), a friend, Annelise Pratt, to whom the book is dedicated, gave me the names of some people with whom I could talk. (Of course most Danes do speak English.) I decided to fly over, but the time was so limited: The book was due at the publisher and, as always happens, I had agreed to speak at some workshop, and I just had a very tight schedule. So I called my travel agent who gulped because the airfare—for somebody not making a reservation a month in advance—was horrendous. I went to Copenhagen for three days and did everything I felt I needed to do and came back and finished the book."

The dust jacket of *Number the Stars* carries the round gold seal that designates it as a John Newberry Medal winner, and there is a shiny gold star of David that dangles from a broken chain that seems to be floating through space. Behind the star and chain is a photograph of a beautiful blonde girl in a flowered dress. "That cover design," says Lowry, "was almost accidental. When the publisher was about to produce a cover, . . . they called me and asked if I would provide the illustrator with a more detailed description of the girl. Usually they don't have consultation on the cover. I said, 'Sure,' and, in thinking about it, I went back to my old files. I used to be a photographer of children, and I had this old photograph of a little Swedish girl. I said, 'Give this to the illustrator because this is what Annemarie Johansen should look like.' They called back almost immediately and said, 'We want to use the photo, so I tracked down the girl's parents to get their permission. They laughed and said, 'You'll have to ask her; she's twenty-three now.' . . . This girl," Lowry said., "could be my daughter or me when I was young."

Number the Stars is also one of the few books about the occupation of Denmark that does not include the apocryphal story of the Danish king, Christian, who supposedly decided to wear the yellow star of David that the Nazis mandated for all Danish Jews. According to that story, he appeared on the balcony of the palace with a star on his uniform and, within hours, most of the population of Copenhagen, Jewish and non-Jewish, followed his lead, in effect stymieing the Nazis in their search for Jewish citizens. "Early on in the book when I tucked away a yellow dress in a trunk, it was because I was going to have Mrs. Johansen remove the yellow dress at some climactic moment, and cut out yellow stars for her Christian children's clothing. But when I discovered through careful research that the story of King Christian never happened, it was very disappointing to me, because I wanted it to happen, and I had that yellow dress all folded and prepared. But I couldn't pretend it did happen."

Again and again people have asked Lowry why she omitted the King Christian story from this novel. When she explained to an audience in Los Angeles "that it hadn't happened, a woman came up to me afterwards, just anxious and eager to tell me that it had happened, and she could prove it to me because she had read it in *Reader's Digest!* The nearest I can guess is that pictures of King Christian show him wearing these sort of pseudomilitary outfits, with various decorations, as he rode out on his horse each morning. Photos from that time are black and white, but probably one of those decorations was yellow, and so, through the years, people have made the assumption that it was a star of David. But when I went to Denmark I found that Danish Jews had never been required to wear stars, except for the five hundred or so who were captured and put into camps. The Danish Jewish population, when they were on the streets of Copenhagen, didn't have to wear the stars."

Lowry says that an incident similar to the King Christian story "did happen in the Netherlands. The Dutch Christian population took it upon themselves to wear yellow stars, very briefly, but they were threatened with terrible reprisals" and the revolt ended.

Perhaps Lois Lowry's most insightful comments during our interview were those about herself. Surrounded by healthy plants, stacks of books on gardening, and containers full of knitting needles of every size, she says, "My problem in life is not having strong opinions about most things. That's not," she adds, "because I'm stupid or I don't think, but it probably accounts for why I write fiction. I'm able to see things from every point of view and from everybody's perception." She is open both to multiple ideas and to the many people at schools and libraries who want to hear her speak. "What happens," Lowry explains, "is they call and say, 'Can you come to Indianapolis in February?' I look at my calender and say, 'Sure.' And then it gets to be late January and I say to Martin [her companion of many years], 'Why did I say I was going to Indianapolis? I don't want to go to Indianapolis.' He listens and doesn't say anything. Then I go . . . and I come back and say, 'Oh, they were so nice; I loved it.' They are always good people, and as a children's writer you never face a hostile audience.

"Like most writers," says Lowry, "I chose this profession, or it chose me, because I was a very introverted person, quite happy to sit all alone and commune with my typewriter and my thoughts. But to achieve any success, you have to go out there and make speeches. That was terrifying at first, but, to my surprise, I feel comfortable."

That is exactly the way her thousands of readers—all over the world and in many languages—feel when they are reading the work of Lois Lowry.

BOOKS BY LOIS LOWRY

NOVELS
(All hardcovers published by Houghton Mifflin, in Boston):

A Summer to Die, 1977. Bantam, 1979.
Find A Stranger, Say Goodbye, 1978. Dell, 1990.
Anastasia Krupnik, 1979. Bantam, 1984.
Autumn Street, 1980. Dell, 1986.
Anastasia Again! 1981. Dell, 1982.
Anastasia At Your Service, 1982. Dell, 1984.
Taking Care of Terrific, 1983. Dell, 1984.
The One Hundredth Thing about Caroline, 1983. Dell, 1985.
Anastasia, Ask Your Analyst, 1984. Dell, 1985.
Us and Uncle Fraud, 1984. Dell, 1985.
Anastasia on Her Own, 1985. Dell, 1986.
Switcharound, 1985. Dell, 1991.
Anastasia Has the Answers, 1986. Dell, 1987.
Rabble Starkey, 1987. Dell, 1988.
Anastasia's Chosen Career, 1987. Dell, 1988.
All About Sam, 1988. Dell, 1989.
Your Move, J.P, 1990. Dell, 1991.

Anastasia at This Address, 1991.
Number the Stars, 1991. Dell, 1990.
Atta-boy, Sam!, 1992.

NONFICTION

Here at Kennebunkport (photos by Lowry; text by Frederick H. Lewis).
 Brattleboro, Vt.: Durrell Publications, 1978.

Susan Kenney

THE state of Maine resounds and abounds with places—Deer Isle, Pretty Marsh, Blue Hill Bay, Eggemoggin Reach, Seven Hundred Acre Island, and Penobscot—where the literary fiction and mysteries of Susan Kenney, who teaches at Colby College, are often set.

Kenney's mystery novels—all of them well-plotted good reads—feature her indomitable English professor-turned-sleuth, Roz Howard, and Howard's long-distance, aristocratic, Scottish lover,

Alan Stewart. Her literary fiction consists of *In Another Country,* six interconnected short stories, which won the Quality Paperback Book Club's New Voices Award for the best first novel of 1984, and the largely autobiographical *Sailing,* about her husband's successful bout with cancer. Both of these are unsentimental and harrowing acknowledgments of the unexpected incursion of serious illness into the lives of the unsuspecting, and both deal with those survival skills that emerge in the face of disaster. Sara, the heroine of *In Another Country,* is a woman whose life has been marked by the early death of her father, her mother's madness, and the protracted illness that threatens her husband's life; Bill, in *Sailing,* is a quiet college professor with an unremitting inner strength.

Although an admirer of her literary fiction, I was most interested in interviewing Susan Kenney as a writer of mysteries. Her first, *Garden of Malice,* is distinguished by what *Publishers Weekly* called its "delectable descriptions of the gardens, so real you can almost smell them, and in the sudden, shocking contrasts she is able to create by imaginatively juxtaposing beauty and terrible cruelty." That first book was followed by *Graves in Academe,* where the ever-resourceful Roz finds herself attracted to three men on campus—Luke Runyon, the "insidiously charming" college dean; Thor Grettirsdottir, a vegetarian sculptor who should, according to Icelandic tradition be named Grettirsson; and Rick Squires, a curious student. In this novel, the idyllic quality of the picture-postcard New England campus of Canterbury College is seriously imperiled when various members of the English department are attacked or murdered in ways that parallel Roz Howard's course syllabus for "English 21A, Survey of English Literature, A.D. 800–1666," and the required readings from *The Norton Anthology of English Literature,* Volume One.

Kenney says that her most recent mystery, *One Fell Sloop,* where Roz and Alan discover a dead body lying on the beach, "was a harder book to write because it took longer and I had my time interrupted. When I finally finished the book and I realized how long it had taken and how hard it had been, a friend reminded me, 'This is the first book you've written while you were teaching.' For each book up until this one, I had had some time where I could write the bulk of it," but while Kenney was finishing *One Fell Sloop* she taught full time at Amherst College.

Kenney's problem with this third mystery, she explained, was that "the gender thing kept overwhelming the mystery part. And . . . I had forgotten [when I started to write] what [Alan Stewart] was like and what he talked like and what he sounded like, and I had to get all that back again, because it had been five or six years" since she had worked with this character. "Fictional characters are not like real people—you can't just take up where you left off; that's the scary part. You have to go back. So I reread *Garden of Malice* and tried to get everything back, to make him consistent."

One of the most interesting things about a series of novels where the same characters reappear is that the characters take on a life of their own. As several of the writers interviewed for this collection make clear, this happens with characters in every kind of novel. But to sustain several fictional lives over the course of three distinct novels seems especially challenging. Kenney says, "The real problem was that Stewart didn't have a life. Well, maybe he did have a life, and *that's* the problem, because I didn't even know what that life had been. So I spent a lot of time making up what had happened, and my editor ended up cutting most of it out. It was too much background, I think, but I had to do it. . . . I had to examine their relationship—this kind of long-distance thing—and what they were going to do with it, and now I feel pleased that I can just go back to the two of them because . . . they've worked it out." This includes "the way Roz reacts, even though she's sort of deluded about Alan's masculine, condescending, overbearing ways. He means well, but he's directive. He doesn't have to be that way, but he spends most of the book not knowing what hit him."

Roz is kind of testy too, I suggested. "Yeah, cause she's been on her own for a while. I think she's a conflicted woman who is not a feminist in any heavily politicized sense. She's political in the sense that she took sides on various issues, but she's really an academic . . . sort of like me."

Roz is also reminiscent of Sara in *Sailing,* a woman, admits Kenney, who "becomes overbearing and directive, but for very good reasons." She is forced by her husband's illness to deal constantly with doctors, many of whom seem to be using him as a guinea pig for painful and unsuccessful treatments, and with hospitals and treatments that are both inefficient and inhumane.

In some ways, Kenney said, *"One Fell Sloop* is the underside of *Sailing,"* and she points out that water is the key to the connections between the two books. "In *One Fell Sloop,* the sailing and the boating are just background setting. I don't think there is much symbolic weight to that although the couple has a little boat and that is an irritant. But what's wrong with their relationship—and also with Alan—is that he responds to being on a boat, and being on the ocean, by controlling Roz." In *Sailing* the scenes where the husband is on the lake, and sailing finally on the ocean, have a heavier symbolic content.

However, Kenney said, in both cases, "men just take over. My husband is a prince; he's very mild-mannered, and he's not at all a directive person. He's a real academic intellectual, and he likes to let people find out their own way. But in a boat, something happens. He gets bossy, . . . a personality change. And I tried to have that be part of Alan's character." Unlike Bill in *Sailing,* or Kenney's own husband, Alan doesn't need to undergo a personality change. "Alan is already that way. To begin with, he's a Scottish aristocrat."

Kenney feels that the "control issue in sailing is always interesting. The female character in *Sailing* assumes that her husband relinquishes control after he becomes ill, but he really doesn't; she doesn't get control. The tension of that book is that control goes back and forth. That is the conflict, and at one point I made it into a series of waves. The point I wanted to make, or the way I wanted *Sailing* to finish, they would finally understand the other person's point of view and accept the way the other thinks. It's the same with the characters in *One Fell Sloop*. They do, on a much more superficial level, understand each other's point of view—the push-pull" of all relationships.

Kenney herself sailed "up until I got progressively more and more frightened of ocean sailing and until I just couldn't deal with the stress anymore. Then we got a bigger boat about five years ago, and it had better equipment. I realized that I wasn't afraid anymore, because I felt I could start the engine and get out of there. And then I discovered I just found it very tedious, if you're not sailing the boat. And I'm still too timid to sail a big boat because I've never had the experience of skippering. I was always crew," an issue that arises for the female characters in both *Sailing* and *One Fell Sloop*. "But both of the women in these two books [like sailing more] than I ever did. If it's possible, they know more about sailing than I did, because I had to do research so I could get beyond my own limitations."

I asked Kenney whether she thought that the fear of sailing or of open spaces was somehow gender-linked or if sailors become more afraid as they age. "The fear isn't a feminist issue. It's just a fact that there are very few female sailors who actually take charge and are in charge of bossing the men around. Are any female captains on the America's Cup? I read an article just the other day about the first woman on the Olympic trials team, the first, and the Olympic sailing events go back quite a ways! For the first time they've got a woman skippering."

In Kenney's case, at least, fear of sailing is not age-related. "I was always afraid, and the bigger the boat and the less control," the worse it was. "I don't know that the fear quotient grows with time. It seems to me that it grows according to how much space there is: In a smaller boat, on a lake, you can always see the shore. . . . I think [the concept that open spaces become closed spaces for women] is really fascinating. I've never really understood this, but I do feel that way about airplanes. I've always been petrified of airplanes. In *Sailing*, when the female character says she's afraid of airplanes, the psychiatrist makes some sort of flippant remark that it's claustrophobic, and maybe she's afraid of being surrounded by air, but that's what gets me—this little bitty plane and this big air!"

For the husband, Bill, in *Sailing,* the ocean, where there are no visible perimeters, becomes a freer space. In spite of the somewhat ambiguous ending of that book (in the last paragraphs the husband, still very ill, sails off alone and his survival is somewhat in question), Kenney had never considered changing the ending to make it clearer that the husband survives. "Some people have insisted that I write a sequel. But I won't do that. If I do, people will know how *Sailing* came out and I don't want to touch that." Although "people really want to know what happened to Bill [and to Kenney's own husband], they should read the book the way I meant to write it. What specifically happens to Bill is not important, because the real ending is the resolution of two people's points of view" and what they learn about their own resources.

About her own husband's struggle with cancer, she believes that "in living with it, you become disabused of the idea of a cure. But then that just becomes irrelevant. . . . My husband has, in fact, had cancer since 1977, so now he's had it almost fourteen years. At the beginning, the doctors talked about a cure, and you'd hear about 100 percent to 0 percent—you're either dead or you're cured. Well, I'm here to tell the tale that you can be neither and go on for a very long time. When the doctor in *In Another Country* says, '*Perfect* is the enemy of *good,*' that [dialogue represents] the first time anybody said anything that really made sense to me about what we had gone through up to that point." Her intention in *Sailing,* she added, was to show that cancer is "awful, but it might not be as bad as you think. The important thing is to make it so real that people will feel that they've gone through it and survived.

"I had quite a bit of mail when that book came out, and I still do get letters about it, maybe once a month. But the people who are depressed by it probably don't write to me; maybe the sample is skewed. The people who reviewed it seemed to expect that it would be depressing and found that it wasn't. Sometimes

I reread chapters, when I'm doing readings, and I find myself chuckling and thinking, 'This is pretty funny,' but I don't remember writing it for that reason. I don't think cancer is something you would pick to write about unless you had to. . . . It wouldn't be my choice of subject if I hadn't been handed it. It sort of chased me down. I really felt that I had to write this book: I didn't choose the subject; it chose me."

Somewhat surprisingly, Susan Kenney said, "I have a feeling that I have more mysteries in me than other books, because that is what I do for recreation in my head. The next mystery," she says, "is already plotted out. In fact, I could probably sit down tomorrow and write the first several chapters. I'm set to go, because I have Roz and Alan settled down. They go to a ski resort in the next one, and he's going to be reading a poison-plant book. For years I've thought about what a wonderful setting a ski resort is for all the ways to murder people." (Kenney is not a skier but "an ex-skier who got injured." And even though she will undoubtedly return to the waters of Maine for future novels, she doesn't sail anymore.)

Her dual writing career does not seem to be problematic for Susan Kenney. Most reviewers, she says, "put the mysteries in one category and the other books in another, and so the books get different kinds of attention," although she was surprised that the reviewer of *One Fell Sloop* failed to mention her award-winning literary novels. "I wonder if that reviewer has even read the other novels." The lukewarm review didn't particularly bother her, since "my agent and my editor were both delighted. They said it was great that the book even made it into the *New York Times!*"

The opinions of her readers seem much more important to her. "Lots of people write to me and say, if they've read all of the books, that they don't make any distinction. But then I'll get a letter that says, 'Why do you write mysteries? You're so much better at writing [realistic] novels.' And then I also get letters saying, 'Why do you write this realistic stuff when you write such great mysteries?' " Kenney's response is, "I just write. It's all the same to me, although I do have to contend with this bias against mysteries, and my mysteries aren't just mysteries, at least to my mind. I see the mysteries relating to the other books [in the same way that] I alternate thematically—for instance, *Garden of Malice* has a lot about family and memory in it, and I was literally writing it at the same time as *In Another Country*. I'd work on one book and try to finish a draft, and work on the other, and they were both sandwiched in over a five year period."

Her interest in mysteries "goes back to the Nancy Drew books I read when I was a preteen. My mother was a great mystery buff, and I just went right on to Mary Roberts Rinehart. It's interesting that there are a lot of women mystery writers and a great preponderance of them at the end of the nineteenth century and the beginning of the twentieth."

At the time of our interview, Susan Kenney was working on a literary novel. "I'm still doing research to get enough sense of the subject, and the setting, and the time, so I can go ahead with it. I'm not teaching this year, but I'm not at the stage where I can sit down and write." In fact, "I spent time snapping pictures today because I think that some of it will take place in New York in the 1930s, and I have to recreate the buildings in my head. I think this is part of my academic background: I really do have this sense that I need primary sources; it just won't do to have somebody tell me what it was like then. My mother is a good resource because she lived in New York in the 1930s, and, in some ways, this book is going to be based on her life.

I'm even toying with the idea of making it a cross-genre novel, both fiction but memoir, and I'm trying to sort out the difference. My mother loves this idea because she always wanted to be a writer and something stopped her, and now she says to people, 'I don't have to write up my life; my daughter's doing it.' So my mother reads some of my stuff and she edits, 'This is not the way it happened. What is this? This word is wrong. So-and-so wasn't there. Hmm, this is made up, . . . pretty good too.' "

Susan Kenney

BOOKS BY SUSAN KENNEY

FICTION

Garden of Malice. New York: Scribners, 1983; Ballantine, 1984.
In Another Country. New York: Viking, 1984; Penguin, 1985.
Sailing. New York: Viking, 1988; Penguin, 1989.
Graves in Academe. New York: Viking, 1985; Penguin, 1990.
One Fell Sloop. New York: Viking, 1990; Penguin, 1991.

Anne Rice

IN SPITE OF having written five novels about vampires and the occult, no sense of the supernatural hovers over the gorgeous doll-filled rooms of Anne Rice's violet-colored, 1857 mansion in the Garden District of New Orleans (unless, of course, you count the benevolent ghost of Pamela Starr, who lived there for seventy-five years and continues to haunt the Rice house on First Street). And also behind the electrified, wrought-iron fence, a commonplace in that neighborhood, and the various assistants dressed entirely in black, lives the verbal, intense, highly motivated and well-organized author of *The Vampire Chronicles: The Vampire Lestat, The Mummy or Ramses the Damned,* and *The Queen of the Damned.*

After twenty-seven years in northern California, Rice returned to her birthplace in 1988 with her husband Stan, a poet and expressionist painter whose work lines many of the downstairs walls, and her son Christopher, born six years after the death of the Rices' five-year-old daughter from leukemia. In spite of this tragedy, what you sense around this writer is a celebration of beauty. Even the glassed-in sunroom, where the interview took place, has furniture whose fabric swarms with giant yellow-and-blue peacocks, and a satisfied-looking, stuffed cat languishes on the sofa. Not even the full-sized male skeleton perched on a nearby red velvet chair seems to be threatening.

Anne Rice sips from frequently replenished cans of Tab as she considers your questions. Although it is no secret that *The Witching Hour* (Rice's latest novel about a mysterious organization of psychic investigators, the Talamasca, and the Mayfair family in New Orleans and San Francisco) is part of a 5 million dollar 2-book deal, which has also underscored her power in publishing, Rice says frankly that "it takes some getting used to, after years of struggling, like many other people, to get somebody's attention for five minutes. But I'm aware of it, just as I'm aware of it when it rains." And clearly Rice is enjoying it. The most important thing now, she adds, "is to remain absolutely honest and absolutely pure, and just to ask yourself each time, 'Am I doing just what I really believe I should do?' " and not "in any way to yield to the more seductive aspect of that power.

"At the same time, I think it's every artist's dream to see the vision you want realized, to be able at last to say, 'Could you do the jacket this way?' What author hasn't felt he or she was destroyed by jacket copy on a book or a press release that misrepresented everything? We've all . . . felt we knew better what the book was about than the people who packaged it and sold it, or *missold* it, . . . and you do long for that moment when they will listen to you. Although I'm uncomfortable with the idea of using that power in any way that would be distorted or dishonest," she adds, "I know all about money, and I read all my contracts to the last word."

While the purpose of this collection is to look both at the writing of each author and at the writer herself, this is somewhat complicated in the case of Anne Rice. Under that name she is the author of *Interview with the Vampire* (her first book, about an existential vampire named Louis), *The Feast of All Saints* (dealing with free people of color in New Orleans), *Cry to Heaven* (about eighteenth-century Italian castrati), and the four books in *The Vampire Chronicles*. She also writes fiction about contemporary relationships, rather than vampires and witches, under the name of Anne Rampling (*Exit to Eden, Belinda.*) And then there is Anne Roquelaure (meaning "cloak") who writes, or at least in the past has written, hard core pornography: *The Claiming of Sleeping Beauty, Beauty's Punishment, Beauty's Release*. Rice says, however, that "at this point these voices have blended together. I think that the *Queen of the Damned* and *The Witching Hour* . . . have involved all three voices. And I don't feel any need to write any more pornography; I've pretty much completed what I wanted to do with the three *Beauty* books.

"I really didn't have any mechanism for shifting gears; I just slip into the material. Long before I was ever published I wrote many, many short stories and tried different novels, and in some ways the Anne Rampling voice was going back to a voice I had experimented with a lot before I'd written as Anne Rice. Writing *Exit to Eden* [as Rampling] helped me write *The Vampire Lestat* as Anne Rice, because I was able to take some of the immediacy I felt I had gotten with Elliot and Lisa [in *Exit*] and bring that to the character of Lestat. That warm[ed] up the Anne Rice voice, which was more remote and was very remote in *Cry to Heaven*."

All of that may be true, but the question for this interviewer was where Rice's obsession with vampires, witches, and castrati—that is, with otherness, difference, and strangeness—originated.

To begin with, Anne Rice reinvented herself in first grade. She had been named Howard O'Brien, after her father, "who didn't even like to be called Howard. He told all his friends at the post office where he worked to call him 'Mike.' I thought Howard was an ugly name and a name that caused people to stare at me; I wanted a pretty, simple name. But my radically liberal parents thought it was wonderfully clever to name a girl Howard. It was part of their attitude toward life. Ironically, they named the next child Tamara, which is a beautiful name. . . . I always felt that they made an error in judgment with me.

"I didn't want people to think I was a weirdo or crazy or a boy; that was disturbing to me. I wanted not to attract attention for that. So when I told the first grade teacher I was 'Anne,' my mother, being this crazy liberal, said, 'If she wants her name to be Anne, put down Anne.' And, in the same spirit in which she named me Howard, she renamed me Anne. It was completely in accord with her principles."

Even after the name change, Rice suffered in grammar school and later in high school, where she thought she "was masculine and weird and different from other girls. Women who are very sexually alive may be afraid that there is something wrong with them. If you grew up as I did at the end of the fifties, . . . there was still so much confusion about what women want and how they feel . . . and all the rules of the game about what you allowed boys to do. I also had a strong interest in male nudity, and wanting to know what men looked like," and all of that "leads you to believe something is wrong with you.

"In any case, most people (not only writers) feel like outsiders. . . . I felt like a gay man for a lot of my life, and I thought that was a fairly common thing for women to feel. But I remember one woman looking at me and saying, 'No, I can't imagine feeling that way.' But I think a lot of women can understand that: I was attracted to men, and yet I felt a bit like a man myself. It's hard for me to talk about this with much passion because I don't care about it now, but I cared terribly when I was twenty.

I was so scared that something was the matter with me. When I was younger I was very frightened."

What seems most relevant to Rice about her childhood is growing up in New Orleans as an Irish Catholic, "in a very strict sort of Catholicism. Yet the Catholicism of the city is distinctly Latin. It's theatrical, filled with images and statues and flowers and processions and festivals, which we associate more with South America or Italy. We were an Irish / German parish, but we were run by an order of Italian priests, and so our great church, St. Alphonso's, looks like a Romanesque church, and it's filled with murals and dazzling stained glass windows. Right across the street is St. Mary's, the German gothic church—the German and Irish immigrants would not go in the same church, even though the Italian priests dealt with both groups." The two churches are standing to this day, "just six blocks from here, right next to each other.

"The influence of the French and Spanish in New Orleans made our Irish Catholicism a bit more flamboyant and Latinized than it would otherwise have been, and I think that contributed to my feeling like an outsider in American life. When I first saw television sitcoms and saw what American life was supposed to be, it was hard to relate that to this world here in New Orleans, the only culturally Catholic city in America. We really don't have the Protestant work ethic here. I mean, this is a decadent, laid-back, inefficient, banana republic–style town. Almost every other city in America [reflects] the Protestant work ethic and the values of the middle class, but New Orleans is visibly a city of the rich and the poor. And when you grow up here, as I did, it's quite astonishing later to discover America." For instance, Rice said, "I don't think I ever knew a Protestant until I went to Texas (except for my Baptist stepmother). . . . And that's the way to understand my work and its otherness and its weirdness."

"My writing is really pre–Protestant Reformation writing. It involves the Devil and God, and good and evil, and saints and magical beings, as the literature did before Martin Luther threw out the cult of the saints, the cult of the Virgin, and the stained glass windows, and before the Protestants after him tried to eradicate the Devil (although Luther believed in him.)"

Rice maintains that American fiction remains profoundly Protestant. "The novels of Anne Tyler and John Updike, for example, are Protestant novels. It doesn't really matter if the [writer] is a Protestant: Saul Bellow's *The Victim* is what I'd call the Great American Protestant Novel, even though it's about Jews and it's by a Jew. But it's fiction about middle-class life, and it's saturated with Protestant values: The ordinary person is what matters; the ordinary person's small moment of illumination is what matters. It's completely middle class, and I have no interest in that."

Rice herself was strongly influenced early on by nonfiction and history: *Lives of the Roman Emperors* and *Lives of the Saints.* "I was a slow reader and didn't read much fiction until I was about fourteen. The two books that influenced me most were *Great Expectations,* which I read in class, and *Jane Eyre,* which I read alone in the library. To this day, those are two of the most powerful influences on my work.

"I didn't discover the Russian writers, Dostoyevsky and Tolstoy, until I was in my thirties, and I was absolutely knocked out by *Anna Karenina.* I go back to it all the time just to remind myself to write everything I want to say about a character. A few years ago," Rice added, "I had one of the most interesting reading experiences of my life. I read Mary Shelley's *Frankenstein* for the first time and I couldn't believe how absolutely wonderful it was, how eccentric, how weird. . . . Of course the introduction to the book told me how people had regarded it as a second-rate work, how—only now—we are realizing its genius. Shelley yielded to the imagination, and to me the book was all about Mary [herself]. The monster was Mary's sexuality, going against everybody when she ran off with Shelley."

There is no rancor when Rice talks about how long it has taken for her novels to gain acceptance, "for the critics to stop saying my novels must be junk," while they continued to praise "outstanding examples of the Protestant novel like Alice Adams's."

It was all upstream [for them to realize] that a novel where everyone is a vampire is just as serious as anything written by Jayne Anne Phillips. . . . For years the most common comments made to me were, 'I avoided reading your book, but one night I picked it up, and boy, was I surprised,' or, 'I didn't want to read your books; someone made me do it, and they were wonderful,' or 'I read *Interview with the Vampire,* and it certainly wasn't what I thought it was going to be.' It's been a long struggle to overcome that [perception] through word of mouth." Rice also feels that "the culture in general is thirsting for Faust and Mephistopheles. It is tired of the small novel of manners—upper-middle-class-man-has-midlife-crisis-in-Ann-Arbor."

In view of her absolute commitment to her own style and subject matter, it was not surprising to find that Anne Rice has equally strong ideas about controlling her own material. "This editing thing is a Protestant issue too," she says. "If you want to succeed in the corporate world or the university world, you really can't be a stoned genius; they're not going to want that," and it translates to the world of publishing with editors who "continually ask, 'Can the book be toned down and rounded off?' . . . I love books to be eccentric and wild and mad. To me, that is what *The Brothers Karamazov* is, . . . and thank God no New York editor got Dostoyevsky against the wall."

As for her own books, "when it comes to editing, I'm very, very resistant. This has not been easy for my editor because she is famous for a hands-on approach to fiction. There have certainly been times when I've expanded or cut or changed something because she has insisted or felt strongly that it was the best thing for the book. But it was never easy for me" because "I edit my own work almost obsessively as I write and as I go through the copyediting stage of the manuscript, and the galleys, and page proofs. And what really interests me is *not* collaborative art; it's the vision of *a* writer. I don't recommend that [other] writers feel this way. Many authors have a wonderful relationship with their editors, and they get a great deal out of it, but there's no room for anybody else but me in [my] books." Rice says that "what angers me more than anything in the world is the pre-sumption that the final stage of any manuscript is somebody else's editing. You see this in many reviews, the [idea] that any-body, whether it's Shakespeare, William Styron, Danielle Steele, Joyce Carol Oates, or Anne Rice, *should* be edited. There's a fore-gone conclusion [among reviewers] that *somebody* else should have taken a blue pencil and cleaned this [book] up. That [idea] is absolutely demeaning and insulting! That's as insulting as say-ing to Pavarotti, 'We're going to take a tape of you singing, "C'eleste Aida," and we're going to dub in another tenor voice where we think you're a bit thin,' or 'We're going to tone you down.' Nobody would dream of doing that. You wouldn't take a film of Baryshi-nikov dancing and artfully cut in shots of someone else's feet and shoulders and arms and hands to make the image better! So why in the hell should anyone take a pencil and change a word I write?"

Rice is also "fully prepared for the critics to continue to com-plain that [the books] need editing. I really don't care, because the readers do not give me that complaint. Not one in a thou-sand has ever said to me, 'Your books are too long.' In fact, people ask, if there are pages I was forced to take out, . . . could they please see those pages?" Commenting about critics who say a book should be shortened, Rice remarks that "seldom are reviewers part of the audience for that book." She does concede that "at this point in my life, more of my reviewers are part of the audience for the books, but in the beginning almost none of them were. . . . So I can't emphasize enough how much I think writers should absolutely ignore reviews. Reviews aren't criti-cism, which comes over the years in theses and dissertations and [scholarly] articles. The shallowness and the lack of integrity, the flippancy, the disregard of newspaper reviewers is simply too great for anyone to take seriously." In fact, says Rice, "that's one of the first things we have to tell young novelists: Don't listen. You will not learn from reviews what you have accom-plished. They will not tell you. All you need to do is look at the reviews that Faulkner and Hemingway got . . . or Virginia Woolf's review of *The Sun Also Rises* where she did not seem to think it was an important book and just dismissed it.

"What I do when I write is instinctive. I'm not particularly good at structuring, and since I've found endings to be rather artificial, I'm not very good at doing them. I seem better at stopping the book—(just bringing the story to a close and actually making my readers very, very angry; they write me furious letters saying, 'How could you do that?')—and then continuing the story in a sequel.

"As young writers, we tend to kill off characters; it's the best way to end something. But, as you get older, you begin to realize you have to do something better." Only when Rice creates characters that she doesn't understand, she admits, do "they die fairly soon in the book, like Nicholas in *The Vampire Lestat*. He represents a type of person that I can't stand. I was trying to show how attractive that kind of person could be, but how ultimately bleak it could be to know someone who is that cynical, that despairing, and that rebellious for the sake of rebelliousness."

Rice also says she sees "the story as bigger than the covers of the book. I frequently see a whole novel [in my imagination] before I even know who is going to tell the story. That was a big problem in *The Witching Hour*. I saw the characters, the sprawling tale, and I wasn't even sure who was to narrate this. Only when I pulled it all together, in about five months' time, did Michael and Rowan [Mayfair] become the third-person narrators. I wasn't even sure until the last minute if Aaron Lightner [a psychic investigator with the power to read minds], this outsider, was going to be the narrator."

In a Rice novel, the characters control the action. They "are strong, manage to accomplish things, and triumph against incredible odds, and that is what fascinates me. I love all my characters. They all represent what I would be if I were that person because I don't write about people that I despise or hate. I don't write from anger. Lestat [in *The Vampire Chronicles*] is certainly my hero" because "he has the capacity to act, without doubt, that I don't have. He is the man of action in me.

"I love my characters for different reasons, but it is much easier for me to write about a male character than a female. It's easier for me to put all of the goodness and openness into a male character, and I don't know why. It troubles me that my women characters tend to be amoral, and they tend to be ruthless, and they tend to have a streak of pragmatism like Gabrielle, the mother of Lestat, or Claudia, the child vampire [in *Interview* who is thus saved from mortal death], or Rowan Mayfair. They are powerful and have a fierce and almost dangerous strength that hurts the male characters. Whether this is a battle in me between the feminine and masculine sides, I don't know. It could be that they are the opposite of what they seem and are being disguised. Deliberately, I don't think about it, but I am sometimes a little politically disturbed . . ." by this battle.

"People have pointed out to me that my characters travel, they move a lot, and I'm very conscious of that because I love the idea of movement; I love using different cities as backgrounds. I tried to get an almost global perspective in *The Queen of the Damned,* a sense of everything happening all around the planet, and I love the idea of characters moving rapidly through space. Gabrielle, the female vampire in this novel and in *The Vampire Lestat* is a wanderer; she's always just passing through." On the other hand, Rice "love[s] houses. Houses have great personalities for me; they have great meaning. This house that I live in, for instance, I used in *The Witching Hour,* and it really is a character in the book."

While it is clear to anyone who spends the morning with Anne Rice that she is tough and clear-sighted about her own value as a writer, it is equally apparent that, unlike the unattractive Nicholas, despair plays no part here. (Her cynicism, as the previous comments testify, has not completely disappeared either!) It seems clear that her rebelliousness as a writer has greatly benefited her readers, but it was also fun to hear that Anne Rice's general sense of entitlement extends to her life as a woman. As she walked me through the gate, Rice recalled one last story that perhaps tells as much as any other about her sense of self and her place in a complicated universe. She laughed and said, "I just thought of something funny. One of the publicists who takes me on tour was talking to an older publicist about whether she should valet-park the car or save money and go find a parking place, and we would then walk to the hall.

"The older publicist said to her, 'Do what a *white* man would do!' And I've thought of this many times—advice from a wonderful woman who is afraid of no one. Do what the CEO would do; just go and *do* it."

BOOKS BY ANNE RICE

NOVELS

As Anne Rice

Interview with the Vampire. New York: Knopf, 1976; Ballantine, 1986.
The Feast of All Saints. New York: Simon & Schuster, 1979; Ballantine, 1986.
Cry to Heaven. New York: Knopf, 1982; Pinnacle, 1983; Windsor, 1988; Ballantine, 1991.
The Witching Hour. New York: Knopf, 1990.
The Vampire Chronicles: The Vampire Lestat, Book 1. New York: Knopf, 1985; Ballantine 1986. *The Mummy or Ramses the Damned,* Book 2 New York: Knopf, Ballantine, 1989, 1991. *The Queen of the Damned,* Book 3. New York: Knopf, 1988; Ballantine, 1989. *The Tale of the Body Thief,* Book 4. New York: Knopf, 1992

As A. N. Roquelaure

The Sleeping Beauty Trilogy: The Claiming of Sleeping Beauty, Vol. 1. New York: Dutton, 1983. *Beauty's Punishment,* Vol. 2, New York: Dutton, 1984. *Beauty's Release,* Vol. 3. New York: Dutton, 1985.

As Anne Rampling

Exit to Eden. New York: Arbor House, 1985; Dell 1986.
Belinda. New York: Jove Publications, 1988.

Sharon Olds

THE POET Sharon Olds, carrying two large teas with milk ("I forgot long ago that sugar existed'), came rushing down the hall at New York University to her purplish pink, windowless office For someone inspired by visual images, the cell-like quality of this space seemed to bother her not at all. She pointed to the Pierre Bonnard print on the wall behind her chair (a painting of a window) and to a small wooden toy window that sat on the corner of her desk. She chose the purply walls too, she said: "Better than if it had been painted this way behind my back."

Sharon Olds, many of whose poems are about a drunken, abusive father and a mother who "wept at / noon into her one ounce / of cottage cheese, praying for the strength not to kill herself," has been called the poet for the 1990s. Although she was not published until 1980, when she was thirty-eight, her third book, *The Dead and the Living,* won the National Book Critics' Circle Award. She has also won a fellowship from the Guggenheim Foundation and a grant from the National Endowment for the Arts. The reason for her enormous success is that in her hands, even trauma of the worst kind results in self-affirmation.

While Olds's intensely confessional material is, as she would say, *apparently* autobiographical, she guards that separation between the actual circumstance and the poetic expression of it with determination and honesty. In agreeing to an interview she said immediately, "I'm happy to be asked any question on earth. I just didn't want to be speaking to you under false pretenses because there are a lot of questions that other people do ask me that I'm not able to answer exactly as they are being asked. I'm happy to talk about anything," she adds, but "I don't talk about my personal life or my personal relationship to these poems. . . . One hopes only to be able to live a life that will bring out the best poems that one can write, whatever they will be."

Olds believes that she is conducting an experiment "to maintain . . . as full as possible separation between the two lives— the actual personal and the public"—and "to keep them as far apart from each other as possible. It's definitely a woman's experiment (though there may be men conducting the same experiment as we speak): Is it possible to protect people from poems and poems from people? To what extent is it possible to be a writer who feels a relative amount of freedom while writing," to maintain her privacy? "We don't know, as we haven't written the unwritten poems yet, if there are young poets who will be having to make similar decisions . . . about their own work and how to handle it. . . . We talk a lot about this in a workshop I teach across the hall and at Goldwater Hospital for the Severely Physically Disabled, about questions of the personal or *apparently* personal nature of one's writing. These are questions that I am very interested in and I think about all the time."

Sharon Olds says that she doesn't "make up the images; they come to me, because I can't make a poem like a cake. . . . Poems come through one to a certain extent, maybe out of the collective unconscious. And to protect those sources might mean wanting not to talk about family, except in general terms, to pretend almost that it's not an issue." That strategy, she feels, might make "it possible to write poems that otherwise one would not be able to write or that you might never show to anyone."

Even if some intensely personal poems are never shared, Olds says, "they have an effect on the next thing we write." Her point is that "speaking in a poetic voice tends to have a cumulative effect of relief and allows the poet to produce poems that might be possible to publish in some decade and not in another or to deal with subjects that it would be possible to discuss more easily at some times than others. One would, I guess, have to have great confidence and faith, and perhaps knowledge, about how one works inside, to feel free to talk about everything." Since Olds's next book is entitled *The Father,* a book of poems which she says is about "the illness and death of a father, . . . poems written for several years after that event," these questions will undoubtedly arise again.

Olds was happier to talk about what she considers her other subjects, which she says are "very small, or *apparently* very small: a skinned knee—the skinning and the healing and the relationship between the two—and the real knee on that real being. It's likely in a poem of mine to *be* a real knee on a real being, not a general knee or an ideal knee. In a way, I want to stay away from large concepts. I don't mean that I want to force the poem away from large concepts if the skinned-knee poem ends up going towards a very large concept, as long as it's going there. I don't want to head [it] in a direction of smallness or a direction of largeness. That sounds as if I feel that the poem is virtually written in my head or body by the time I notice that it's there. It is half formed, although I don't mean that in any mystical sense at all."

I commented that many writers, poets or otherwise, consider themselves to be conduits for characters and stories that have their own momentum and direction. "I would think that [these subjects and ideas] are living their mute life," Olds responded, "and I am hoping to say them and sing them. Some I sing in very plain music that's hardly distinguishable from very plain saying. I translate them from real existence into papery existence or from the real existence of a song in the air." At this point, Olds, who seemed always to want to understand questions and her responses to them in very specific, orderly fashion, asked herself, "Why do that? How not [to] want to would be the question, . . . how not [to] want to sing everything. Of course, not everything one would see in the street on the way here [in Greenwich Village] one would know how to sing. . . . Maybe any singing in an attempt at beauty is wrong, but I think that our desire to understand the elements of something, and to understand where there is order and where there isn't, is passionate. So perhaps for some poets the desire to sing something into a different kind of being might just be an effort to understand it, to see order and honor its orderliness and disorderliness and its truth, whatever it is."

With her whimsical black and white barrette holding back her shoulder-length, graying hair, Olds mused about who she considers a poet and decided that she "mean[s] potentially everybody. I suppose I'm really talking about . . . this specialized human, but I'm not thinking male or female when I say that. I'm not thinking old or young, I'm not thinking poets who have had readers and poets who haven't had readers. I'm thinking of everybody, because everyone is really a poet. It's just a human skill like dancing. . . . Every three year old dances in one way or another, and they would as adults if it wasn't taken away. I feel that way about poetry. It's very hard to find a person who never wrote a poem unless they so lacked education they weren't able to, but then they might have [used] an oral tradition that was . . . just as much poetry." Olds remembers the poet Muriel Rukeyser saying to a class in poetry appreciation at the 92d Street YMHA in New York City that poetry "has existed in every culture that has ever existed, and if it didn't exist here, someone would invent it."

When I asked Olds why she herself persisted in this genre, as opposed to writing fiction, she said, "I've thought a lot about why people are fiction writers instead of poets or poets instead of fiction writers. I look at a lot of poetry and see a narrative; that's why I feel we can't entirely distinguish the two in terms of who wants to tell a story. I look at a lot of fiction and see gorgeous prose, so we can't really talk about decorated or undecorated language, or elaborate or simple language. The only thing we can look at, I think, is the line. Prose," she explained, "has the sentence, and poetry has the sentence and the line. (Although some poetry doesn't have the sentence, it just has the phrase and the line.)

"As a teenager, I used to write fiction, and I was very interested in narrative and in description. I was mildly interested in character, but I really didn't understand people very well, . . . and [so] I found I told lies when I wrote fiction: My characters would get their wishes and their wishes would come true in ways that were not believable. For me, fiction was a place where wishful thinking could have some effective results. For my young heroines—dark haired, very nearsighted, odd-looking, alienated, passionate young women—dreams would come true by the end of the story. Or, in an equally mechanical way, their dreams wouldn't come true, and they would die. Once I'd gotten my own measure as a fiction writer, I thought I could fix it by just turning that all upside down, having it all be bad instead of good."

Olds feels that she doesn't "have a very subtle sense of the relationship between literal truth and the truth of art in fiction, and I have absolutely no interest in inventing characters. I know that it's much more subtle than that, that a character is perhaps not even invented, that perhaps characters are combined. Or they may be as close as one can get to one or two actual people." Olds stressed that she also sees novels "as alternate worlds [that exist] within this actual world, . . . and I see poems as more like actuality or reality (quite a mad theory that I'll wish I hadn't even mentioned), a small reality made into another form, perhaps not for transport, but maybe for translation. Short-story writers or long-story writers have this amazing imagination, but poetry requires something other than this." Olds feels that she lacks something fiction writers have, "controlling me towards the truth as I move along in the telling. For me, the [poetic] line does that [controlling]. I'm sure I still lie and the whole question of trying not to be deeply false in one's writing and to be accurate (whether autobiographically or not) is still a big issue for me."

The line she loves so much becomes "like the plank between cliffs. When I look at that bookcase [painted white and totally empty] it's deeply satisfying to me. The lines that form a grid say, 'There's enough stability here in this grid that you could load me up with things and I will hold them, . . . even though in a poem, what the poem has to hold may spill over one side. Certainly my poems don't look like stanzas, like that bookcase, but the grid of order behind it is a very beautiful thing to me. It's like the idea of order, or the skeleton. It works."

In prose, Olds explained, "the sentence doesn't have that [idea of order] because it just bounces off the right-hand margin back to the left-hand margin. Perhaps the look of prose doesn't satisfy my sculptural lust. But a poem has a body or it has half a body. It's like the right-hand half of a Rorschach. As a little kid I looked at poems and I just loved the way they looked, and then I heard them and I loved the way they sounded. There was order."

I asked if poets had what Olds called a "particular sensitivity," and she said that "a lot of people who become poets probably have pretty sharp senses. That might be true of fiction writers as well. Someone told me that there is one poet for every 100,000

Americans, but if everyone who had ever written a poem was included, there would have to be close to 100,000 poets for every 100,000 people." She wondered about those who write poems, but who are not going to regard themselves as poets. "I think for those one-poem poets . . . something has happened that ordinary forms of discourse don't satisfy. At times of birth and love and death, at times of great need or when [a] new person [is] arriving or an old or new person [is] leaving," we need the "kind of repetition which has something to do with rhythmic nature: birth and sexuality and death, and death and birth and sexuality, that beautiful repeated emphasizing that is one thing that distinguishes poetry from prose."

Olds was serious when she said she "dreams of a project that would bring poems into the supermarket, where they would be free of charge and next to the *National Enquirer*. They'd have to be carefully chosen, poems that would be interesting and accessible to those of us who are standing there with our carts." She recalled a time when she wanted to use the "strange" word *quincunx* in a potential supermarket poem, and "I thought the woman with the cart in front of me wouldn't know it. I hadn't known the word until I was playing Dictionary. I didn't write the poem for a while because I didn't want [anyone in that supermarket line] to look at a poem title and say, 'Ugh, I have to go to college before I can understand poetry,' and because the accessibility of poetry to its readers, various poetries to their potential readers—and of my poems in particular—is important to me. But I finally wrote the poem because I just couldn't resist; I was in love with this image. It's a poem called 'Quincunx of Jujubes.'

"It's heartbreaking when poetry is kept from so many people who could use it, and like it, and then write it themselves." Olds's ideas about the distribution of free poetry are in part motivated by her memories of herself as a young reader of great poetry. "I didn't really have a sense that [these poets] once lived. I thought perhaps they were invented. It wasn't until I was in my midforties that I suddenly realized that Emily Dickinson had been alive in her body, and when she took off her shoe and sock, her foot was naked and she could step on the floor with it. I nearly fainted! I thought these poets were some other kind of being, and I didn't connect the poems I made with what they made: They were great and I was what I was, making these little things that had, superficially, certain resemblances to these beautiful beings. . . . I loved these poets."

Olds laughed. "I never really thought of this before, but they were idealized beings, grownups, and yet they were playing, but they were playing brilliantly, and it made me very happy." She says that now she can "go through the *Norton Anthology* and look at Emily Dickinson and look at Whitman and look at Donne and look at Muriel Rukeyser and look at Herbert and each one you know as though you lived down the block [from them] and you see your friend coming. You know it's your friend, although you can only see an arm and a leg; you still know them."

Even though some of the poets that she especially likes— Adrienne Rich, Lucille Clifton, C. K. Williams, Jean Valentine, Philip Levine, Galway Kinnell—write about an enormous variety of subjects, Olds herself is usually thought of as a confessional poet in the manner of Robert Lowell, Sylvia Plath, and Anne Sexton. "That word *confessional* has always interested me because of my upbringing as an Episcopalian. I knew that we were exactly like Catholics except for a few things: We ate meat on Fridays, and we had no one to confess our sins to and be given some task to do, which sounded like repeating poems as far as I could tell. So I do think *confessional* is a very interesting term, but I would like to offer an alternative vision. It seems to me that a confession is something that you feel bad about, something that you've done that is wrong, that you need forgiveness for, or that you feel you need forgiveness for. Confession seems to me to be [related to] sin. . . . But I do not think that writing apparently personal poetry, which is what people seem to be calling confessional poetry, has to do with wrongdoing and asking for forgiveness. So every time I hear the term I go on my little campaign trail. I think it's good for us if we can rethink our terms. I say *apparently* because nobody knows if a poem is per-

sonal or not unless the poet says, 'I wrote this poem about my
. . . whatever.' Then, if you believe the poet, you feel that you
know this was an autobiographical poem. Otherwise, you don't
really know that."

When asked about why there is currently so much confessional poetry, Olds says, "We have a terrible fear that we may
be a bad experiment, . . . that [humans] have not been such a
good idea for the life of the earth, and that we are going to take
it all with us. We need to get to know our species in a hurry.
. . . We need to know how bad we are, and how good we are,
what we are really like, how destructive we are, and that all this
often shows up in families. The more we learn about families,
the more we learn about human nature—about strength and
positive things, and weakness and negative things. I feel there is
actually a force for self-knowledge, driving us in our art to see
ourselves more clearly and to better equip us to fight our tendencies to be dangerous."

Like many of the writers in this collection, Sharon Olds feels
that not to write would be the hardest job: "Silence," she said,
"is difficult; silence is hard; silence is painful. I find singing to
be far less painful than silence. But the creative experience of
poetry is always difficult. An image I've used sometimes is trying
to transfer a very, very overeasy egg from a pan to a plate without breaking the yolk."

She thinks, too, that an audience is "very important for the
unconscious, for this joy and companionship called writing. You
know, there's this strong family feeling among poets, and knowing there are other poets out there, or other readers, is a bless-
ing. If I go to a community, I know that some of the people in
the audience will be young writers. We belong with each other;
we're poets; we're members of that odd tribe.

"I think, to a poet, the human community is like the community of birds to a bird, singing to each other. Love is one of
the reasons we are singing to one another, love of language itself,
love of sound, love of singing itself, and love of the other birds."

Books by Sharon Olds

POETRY

Satan Says. Pittsburgh: University of Pittsburgh Press, 1980.
The Dead and the Living. New York: Knopf, 1984.
The Matter of This World. Nottingham, Eng.: Slow Dancer Press, 1987.
The Gold Cell. New York: Knopf, 1987.
The Sign of Saturn. London: Secker and Warburg, 1991.
The Father. New York: Knopf, 1992.

Lucille Clifton

WHEN "a wonder, a city of a woman," comes striding across the stage in her wool knit red dress and black leggings, ready to talk about her "big, free, mighty, magic, never been enslaved" *hips,* you know that Lucille Clifton is in town and ready to read poetry! And no words could be closer to the truth than those she reads from "what the mirror said": this African-American poet, mother of six, grandmother of newborn twin girls and several mischievous boys, writer of twelve books for children, and distinguished professor of humanities at St. Mary's College (in Maryland) is indeed "a wonder, a city of a woman [with] a geography of [her] own, . . . not a noplace anonymous girl." As the poem says, "mister, . . . somebody need a map to understand you."

The afternoon I interviewed Lucille Clifton she was scheduled to read at Trinity College in Hartford, Connecticut, and the campus was abuzz with excitement. Every other door seemed to have a flier announcing her appearance at 8:00 P.M. that night. But our own conversation initially was about her other life, as the creator of a character called Everett Anderson, a boy about six or eight. As she said, "a lot of people know me as a children's author, but generally those same people do not know me as a poet." Since Clifton started to write about Everett in 1970 and was still doing it in 1983, I asked her what compelled her to write seven books about him. "I teach a course called Racism and Sexism in Children's Books," Clifton said. "And it seemed to me obvious that American children's literature ought to reflect American children, and . . . traditionally it has not reflected *all* of American children. And I wanted to write about a little boy, about a black child, not unlike my boy. (I have two sons and four daughters.) I wanted to write about a little boy who was poor and about someone who, although he had no things, was not poor in spirit. He's full of love, and he and his mother live well together. They don't have a traditional family, but then lots of kids don't. I wanted to write about that kind of child, since sometimes children who are quite poor feel that there's something [wrong] about *them*."

Clifton said that she has lived in the projects, and it was crucial for her to have Everett live there. "A project is not an apartment. Nobody *wants* to move in, you know. People are not in apartments trying to get *into* the projects, but people in projects are trying to get into apartments. Even so, there are children there, and they ought to be reflected. This seemed to me obvious though sometimes people think it is a new concept."

"Now," Clifton said with obvious satisfaction, "people know

Everett Anderson well." And she was emphatic in her answer to my question about audience. "The audience for these books is the same audience that is there for all other children's literature. We have *Black Beauty,* and lots of people don't live on horse farms! So, clearly, literature transcends the setting of the content."

Clifton also mentioned two of her other books, *My Brother Fine with Me* and *All Us Come across the Water.* "People speak to me about those all the time, as if they cannot read those books. But I don't see why. Nobody speaks iambic pentameter verse, and they don't talk to me about that. And they read *Pecos Bill,* they read *Uncle Remus,* they read all kinds of things that don't have standard, written, formal English. And no one wonders what the audience is for that. Teachers talk about how they would like to read my books to their classes, but they don't have many black people, or they talk about how to introduce multicultural literature into classes when they have mostly white kids. These same teachers read books about bears and bunnies to their kids. And if they will deal with other species, surely they can deal with the human species. See, these are made up problems. My audience," she repeated, "is that audience which reads children's literature. Now, how they wish to define themselves—and if others wish to feel themselves excluded from the experience of Everett Anderson—that's their problem. I do not think of myself as excluding anyone from knowing about and feeling for the black American experience" and from being part of it.

Clifton feels that this discussion of audience relates to underestimating what children can understand. "Adults don't understand everything they read; . . . they don't get everything either. I expect people to get what they can. It may be that I, in writing, don't get everything that's there, everything a reader could find. People ask me all the time, 'What age do you write for?' I haven't a clue. How do I know what five year old? Which eight year old? Those questions seem to underestimate kids too much, . . . not to respect them enough."

She is pleased, however, with how well the illustrators for the

Everett Anderson books, Ann Grifalconi and Jan Spivey Gil-christ, have captured the actions and the feelings of her charac-ters. "I've been very fortunate. In children's literature, the people who write the text—if they are not also the artists—have tradi-tionally not had a lot to say about what the illustrations are like." It's changing somewhat now, certainly, but sometime back, one didn't choose the illustrator. The authors often did not see the illustrations until the books were bound. "I've heard other peo-ple say, 'The book in my hand is rarely the book in my head.' An author, I think, has a definite photographic rendition of the words, but an illustrator has a much broader feel for how they illustrate the words. I've been lucky, because what I wanted to get across in Everett Anderson is not just words but the feeling of love in this family."

Clifton added that she doesn't think of "Everett Anderson as poetry although people always tell me it's poetry. But I think it's verse. . . . It's good verse but . . . it's verse. It's strict iambic pen-tameter, rhymed lines, and for most of them I've included Ever-ett's name. I'm also conscious of form. In poetry, I think, form has to follow content. With Everett Anderson I consciously think about what I want to talk about. I have a subject in mind, I have an idea for something, and I work toward that idea. In poetry it's something more than that, something other than that.

"Poetry is the kind of thing that comes both from intellect and intuition. And most poets will admit they are not sure where [their inspiration] comes from. Something drives us toward a particular circumstance so that you choose this chair and not that table, and I don't know if it's exactly that you like the chair better, or you've got six of those chairs and you hate that table. It's none of that. But something draws one, and one learns to trust that. I call it 'the poet outside.' My students crack up when I say that—'What is she, crazy?'—but there is something that draws us, and out of the combination of intuition and intel-lect—intuition resonating with intellect and intellect resonating with intuition—you bring language together. Sometimes when the words come we're surprised, and we think, 'Wow, I'll be darned, did I do that? I'm good!' or 'Phew, I'm lousy.' Verse isn't like that. Prose isn't like that. But poetry comes from us and is more than us. Trying to figure it out is almost an after-the-fact explanation. Poets like to talk about how and why they did stuff," but those discussions generally take place after the poem is written. "I am as surprised as anyone that this continues to happen for me, and with me, and I'm grateful."

That might be, Clifton added, "because I never took creative writing. I'm not a person who came into my work through the academy. We tend in this culture to believe that we need to be trained to do what we do." I asked her if something negative happens to poets who attempt to sharpen their form through workshop writing. "It's fine as long as one remembers that to be a poet is not more important than to write poems. To write poems is more important than to be a poet. And I think the academy tends to make people believe they are preparing to be poets, more than they are preparing to write poems. I do think something negative happens, but you get over it. . . . It's important to get a feel for craft, but it's more important to add craft to the accumulation of experience which goes to make your poems.

"Poetry is a matter of life, not just a matter of language. That's important for poets to remember. It is not just a matter of idea. An English poet, Philip Larkin, said that poetry doesn't start with an idea; it starts with a poem. Nowadays, especially, students get an idea and they start writing, instead of getting an idea and waiting for the poem. You have to be open to mystery. If you are open to it, mystery will come. If you're not, why should it, actually? But I hope that I continue to be open to the world and open to life, and life keeps happening."

Unlike the poetry of many of her contemporaries, Lucille Clifton's work seems forthright, often funny, and always accessible. The audience of women and men at Trinity, for instance, exploded with laughter when she read one of her earthier (and sometimes embarrassing) poems called "wishes for sons." There Clifton "wishes" them not baseball gloves or fast cars, but "a strange town / and the last tampon / . . . [and] no 7–11." And she is probably also the only poet who has written about the onset of menopause in "to my last period." ("well girl, goodbye, / after thirty-eight years . . . you never arrived splendid in your red dress without trouble for me.") There is a subtle political content to many of her poems. Clifton agreed. ("Thank you for noticing," she said.) "I sometimes feel like the Grandma Moses of poets because people never assume that I have layers to my work or that there is an intellectual component. They think I do the 'primitive' act, and they are not allowing to me the complexity that other humans have. And that hurts my feelings sometimes, but I get past it. If you stay there it gets in the way of your work."

Clifton does have poems that are angry. "I have a sense of humor and I laugh about things. But I get angry, so of course poetry comes from there. It would be weird not to be angry at things that would make any human mad." In fact, said Clifton, in her new book, Quilting, she has a poem called "an angry poem." My publisher said, 'Well, that's not a Lucille Clifton poem,' as if I should never have a poem that was angry. But why not?

"I have another poem in Quilting called 'move' and it's about the bombing in Philadelphia and Wilson Goode, and when I read it I say, 'I'm an equal-opportunity poet,' since I talk about the awful thing that was done by a black mayor and a black community against its own. I don't think it is brave enough not to say [anything] when someone has done something exploitative, whoever they are."

Clifton is a poet for whom "everything matters. I like the look of lower case letters, so I tend not to capitalize. I said that to someone once, and they said I was insecure and suggested that perhaps I should see a counselor. But I assured them that I feel really good about myself and that it was only in the context of the poem. I often don't have titles because I'm not good at them, and since I take responsibility for everything that is there, if I don't know exactly what should be there, I don't have anything.

"I try to get my students to understand that language almost becomes visceral. The American oral language is very musical, and if you read a lot and get involved with language, you can get a feeling for how the lines wish to proceed, how the words wish to follow each other, how the sounds work together in a kind of music. I always compose on a typewriter because I need to see it—almost like a score for music."

Clifton reminded me that she does "a lot of persona poems. I speak in voices living and dead, and those personas are not my own, so I want to maintain the integrity, . . . for instance, of Adam and Eve speaking. The character of Eve is not so much Eve, as if she were Lucille. It's Lucille as if she were Eve, and that's a different thing."

While she was waiting for the evening event, Clifton continued to work on a new poem that she would read that night. "I knew the title was 'she, polishing.' Now what the heck does that mean? But I accept the title which came to me—which, for me, is pretty good."

As she read it to me that afternoon, the poem was:

she, polishing the floor
she, scrubbing,
remembering the hen chasing its bloody neck around the room
remembering the feathered bits of flesh
remembering the father's hands transformed and terrible
i was so young. oh i have never gotten over it, she sighs.
we never do. none of us. we never get over anything.

"At one time I thought it should be, 'she polishes the floor.' Well, anybody can say that. I wanted it to be clear that this is continuing, and more than the kind of weird dusting that we periodically do when our friends are coming, . . . which I never do! Now the third line, 'remembering the hen chasing its bloody neck around the room,' was originally 'the chicken chasing its bloody neck around the room,' because when I was a little girl I had seen my father wringing the neck of a chicken, and I tried to remember and return to that experience, which was not for me particularly traumatic. But then I had 'chicken' and 'chasing' . . . ch ch ch. It was an interesting sound of chickens there. And then I thought, wouldn't it be interesting if it's chasing a hen because the hen is also a female, and I changed it to 'she, scrubbing, / remembering the hen,' and that's much better than the chicken chasing its bloody neck. And I had the father's hand simply wringing the neck of a chicken, something farmers do all the time.

"I was trying to build menace, because I wanted to show the edge of menace that often is in ordinary things, the edge of menace that is always around us, and the edge of great joy that is there too. The next line, 'i was so young. oh i have never gotten over it,' I needed because that opens it up for all of us, because this is every 'we.' I do think humans don't get over things even when we think we do, and the poem is about . . . the edge of our trying to make things okay from something we don't even remember is there."

Clifton decided to read the poem that night "and then I'll read [the poems about the] stuff I've never gotten over." These are not limited, she told me, to women's issues, because she believes that "men have pain too; they just have it so buried."

Clifton also talked about myth. "Somebody told me once that what I do is find the human in the myth and the myth in the human.' I plumb the Bible a lot, for somebody who doesn't go to church (although I attend Passover seder every year and went to synagogue for years. I'm quite an ecumenical person). But I think it makes it much more interesting for [biblical characters] to be humans who have been touched by something. It's much more interesting to think of mythic [characters] as human because we, of course, are possibly mythic too, you know. There are," Clifton thinks, "myths that draw us, although we are taught certain ones from the myth canon. But there are others, and it's always fortunate to learn more than you are taught . . . always.

"I always thought that what I was interested in was personal responsibility, the idea that there is in me the possibility for great good and for great evil, and once I recognize that, I can work toward the good. We are all responsible; we are all possible. It seems to me that that's so, and that's what I write about.

One of the joys of being an African-American woman is that I don't buy other people's definitions, and I don't let them get in the way of what I'm writing. I am enriched, my work is enriched, not only by my race, by my experience, but by my children, because those are more worlds that I know. I feel sorry for people that don't know about the worlds I know, because I have an interesting inner life."

Lucille Clifton is amused, "maybe because I have this weird sense of humor, that in February [Black History Month] thousands of black people are running around the country [doing poetry and literary] readings. I tend not to accept things that wish me there [only] because I am a black person. I want to be there because I am a poet, and if I get the feeling that they only want me there because I'm black, I won't go. I go places now where being black is a plus, and that I accept; the realities of what the country is like allow me to accept those invitations. But they've got to make me know that they would have wanted me—a part of contemporary American poetry, not separate from contemporary American poetry—in March or April or even in May."

"By the time I was first published," Clifton said, "which was in 1969, I had been writing for over twenty years, *over twenty years,* and the importance of what I did had to do with the writing. And if I didn't publish, would I write? Well, I already had, for twenty-something years. I like publishing, and I would feel sad if I weren't able to publish any more, but I wouldn't stop writing. Because that, you know, is the nourishing thing."

BOOKS BY LUCILLE CLIFTON

POETRY

Good Times: Poems. New York: Random House, 1969.
Good News about the Earth. New York: Random House, 1972.

An Ordinary Woman. New York: Random House, 1974.
Two-Headed Woman. Amherst: University of Massachusetts Press, 1980.
Good Woman: Poems and a Memoir 1969–1980. Brockport, N.Y.:
    BOA Editions, 1987.
Next: New Poems. Brockport, N.Y.: BOA Editions, 1987.
Ten Oxherding Pictures. Santa Cruz: Moving Parts Press, 1988.
Quilting Poems: 1987–1990. Brockport, N.Y.: BOA Editions, 1991.

NONFICTION

Generations: A Memoir. New York: Random House, 1976.

CHILDREN'S BOOKS

The Black BC's. New York: Dutton, 1970.
Some of the Days of Everett Anderson. New York: Holt, 1970.
Everett Anderson's Christmas Coming. New York: Holt, 1971;
    Holt, 1991.
Everett Anderson's Year. New York: Holt, 1971.
All Us Come Cross the Water. New York: Holt, 1973.
The Boy Who Didn't Believe in Spring. New York: Dutton, 1973;
    Unicorn, 1988.
Don't You Remember? New York: Dutton, 1973.
Good, Says Jerome. New York: Dutton, 1973.
Everett Anderson's Year. New York: Holt, 1974.
The Times They Used to Be. New York: Holt, 1974.
Three Wishes. New York: Viking, 1974.
My Brother Fine with Me. New York: Holt, 1975.
Everett Anderson's Friend. New York: Holt, 1976.
Amifika. New York: H. Holt, 1977.
Everett Anderson's 1-2-3. New York: Holt, 1977.
Everett Anderson's Nine Month Long. New York: 1978.
The Lucky Stone. New York: Delacorte, 1979; Dell, 1986.
My Friend Jacob. New York: Dutton, 1980.
Sonora Beautiful. New York: Dutton, 1981.
Edward Anderson's Goodbye. New York: Holt, 1983, 1988.

Melinda Worth Popham

MELINDA WORTH POPHAM'S second novel, *Sky-water,* which is about a straggly pack of haunted and hunted coyotes in the Sonora desert of southern Arizona who are searching for the mythic place of watery abundance, won the 1990 BUZZ-WORM Edward Abbey Award for EcoFiction, was selected for both 1990 American Library Association lists for best adult and young adult books, and was chosen as one of twenty-nine literary works launching B. Dalton's new Discover Great

New Writers program. Graywolf Press reprinted the novel twice, a mass market paperback was published by Ballantine, and the movie rights were optioned. *But none of it came easy.*

The smiling and very easily delighted Popham, who has sparkling, blue eyes, a soft, modulated, deep voice, and the bony, sensitive hands of an artist, now lives near the beaches of Malibu, California, but she started to write as a young child in her native Kansas City. "It was literally a basement activity for me. My father brought home a Remington so-called noiseless typewriter from his office, and it was installed in the basement. I can remember explicitly, in second grade when you are about seven, being down there typing out stories and making a lot of noise. So I was literally a subterranean child; I was down in the basement or the attic of my own self. . . . I was not on the main floor with other people." She says that her "early writings were always about isolates. They were always about society's rejects, . . . those sort of sad stories that children write. I was really defining my own feelings about how I didn't fit into the world. I saw myself as being an outsider."

These feelings were related to the fact that Popham had a "severe stammer. I was a shy, stammering child, and I could not speak. I even had to develop a subterfuge for how to say the word 'kick' because I couldn't say 'kick.' So I'd say 'push' the ball. You know, you find ways to get around it. I was so tongue-bound, I was so shy, that I think writing really was a way to express this self." Popham says that she now thinks it's clear that "I stammered for reasons having to do with squelching of self. . . If you're locked into being a good girl or a good child, then you squelch yourself, and to express your true self is impossible. It even, literally, becomes impossible to express yourself through speaking, and the stammering was a by-product of my sense of feeling squelched."

She was happier during her college days, although "Chicago felt dead wrong to me. The minute I got out of the car to go attend the University of Chicago as an English major, I just felt my stomach hit my shoes. I felt the wrongness of that place

although I loved the university." But happily she had the opposite experience when she "was first in the desert. I just felt that
a weight had been lifted off me; I was smitten with it."

Like many writers, Popham has thought a lot about her "right
place." In her case, it is the desert, to which she was introduced
by her husband in 1965. His family wintered in Arizona. "They
were from Connecticut, but his brother was a rheumatic-heart
child. During the forties that was what you did if you lived in
the east and your kid had a rheumatic heart; you went to Arizona for the winter. . . . When I met him we went out into the
desert. It was he who got me out there."

What she loved immediately was the sense of space. Popham
emphasizes that she's "always wanted to know some chunk of
nature well and truly. I've always wanted to be conversant with
the wildlife, the flowers, and to really know their names, since
nomenclature means a lot to me. It's like people. Once you know
someone's name, then you identify" with that person. "And,
growing up in the Midwest, which is so leafy," and later "in
Colorado, and wherever I'd gone before, I'd always been overwhelmed by the muchness of everything. I thought, 'How can I
learn the names of all these trees and all these flowers? Where is
the wildlife?' It was overwhelming. When I got to the desert it
was so bone clean and spare. Every single thing has to have its
own access system to whatever available water there is. Everything is sparse, and everything has its own space. For the first
time I had a sense that here is something finite enough so I can
grasp it. I can learn the name of that plant, because it is all by
itself. So the desert inflamed me with a sense of can-do, because
it was manageable. And because I've never lived in the desert, I
can keep responding to it. When you live in a place, you get
tied in with daily what-alls, and I've never had the desert tied in
with driving kids to school or marketing or buying a broom."

In the desert, explained Popham, sometimes "you would see
a lone coyote or a lone saguaro, and it was the loneness of everything out there" that made her feel she could "get hold of this."
Popham added that she "was like a child, insatiable to know

every bone in a horse's body, and to know every part of the horse. . . . I was just inflamed with the desire for knowledge, hungry for it, so it was really the exhilaration of self-education that I was having out there." Popham continues to be fascinated with "what the plants and animals go through to survive. I'm in awe of it. And the coyotes are the supreme example of this act of survival."

Melinda Popham and her husband continue to camp near the "dry arroyos, . . . holed up like the animals under a patch of shade for the day. All my poking around, all my explorations are done from 5:30 A.M. until 8:30 A.M. That's when I'm hiking, making notes, and doing my field observations. In the afternoon, once the sun is climbing down the sky, I can go out for another two or three hours. But from nine to about four, I'm sitting under a tree. I don't like oases. . . . If I am going to be out in the desert, I don't want to be by a perennial creek with sycamores and big leafy trees growing along the banks of a stream. When my husband and I go camping, we are literally out under the sky, not even in a tent. I'm literally on a cot [about two feet off the ground] because snakes can't strike higher than your knee."

This love affair with the desert is no doubt responsible for Popham's ability to portray the coyotes (she pronounces it "ky-oats"), whose landscape it is, as individuals who demand the reader's attention and sympathy. *Skywater,* in fact, is a story of environmental peril told from the viewpoint of these animals, whose water supply has been contaminated by the filings from a copper mine and who are surrounded on all sides by human predators. They are searching for the skywater, "the unfailing, eternal, blue-water place," the ancestral drinking place of the "moon-callers," and are beloved only by two admirable human characters: the eccentric Hallie and her husband, Albert Ryder, who make a living selling rocks and honey to tourists and have lived in a trailer in the middle of the desert for forty years. (This number, which recalls Moses' trek through the deserts and wastelands to Mount Sinai and the temptation of Jesus by the devil in the wilderness for forty days and nights, adds to the novel's allegorical quality. The Ryders' only son, Pete, has been killed in World War II.)

It is the Ryders who name the coyotes after the trash that litters the landscape—Dinty Moore, Kraft, Kodak, Salem, Chieko (named after a Japanese candy bar wrapper), Boyardee, and their enigmatic and orphaned leader, Brand X, who witnessed the slaughter of his siblings and of his father, whose head was impaled as a hood ornament on a hunter's truck. Since coyotes are often considered expendable and believed by many hunters to be "trash" animals, Popham's method of naming her coyotes makes this connection to trash, but immediately humanizes the coyotes for the reader.

Skywater was written first "as a talking animal book," Popham explained. "It was submitted to twenty publishers who turned it down—roundly, soundly, turned it down—and in 1985 it reached the end of the line. I put it aside, very sadly, and then came back to it because I just thought: 'I can't let go of this. I want this book to see the light of day.' I heeded what had been said by the editors who had been good enough to specify their reasons for turning it down, and I listened to them through reading the letters. I always want rejection letters sent to me. I want to know everything that is going on because I am out in California and my agent is in New York."

Popham changed *Skywater* from "a talking animal book" and eliminated the "coyote language, which was centered around water, even though I had even studied Hopi and Zuni language forms to get it to have a sort of southwestern look on the page." Finally, she decided on "a thinking animal book," and just scrapped all of that work. In the original version "for example, Dinty Moore was sort of a campfire storyteller, a teller of Native American trickster tales, and the repository of all of the coyote myths. It became a process of translation and I had to take that language and make it come out through their eyes, ears, and their tails. So *Skywater* is a book that I came back to instead of saying, 'Okay, that book is dead in the water, go on to something else.' I went on to something else, but I was drawn back to *Skywater,* and now of course it's turned out to be a wonderful decision since the original book wasn't nearly the book this is."

It would be impossible not to enjoy Popham's success when you hear her speak so candidly about her first novel, *A Blank Book.* "Like most first novels, it was an emotional autobiography, and I was sort of protected because it was such fantasy. The mother was an out-of-order vending machine, and the father figure was an enormous tortoise that was permanently retracted." You hear her wonderful, infectious laugh when she says, "I'm really lucky that the publisher is no longer in business, and the book is out of print. I think all the old copies are sold, and I think I bought most of them! I'm lucky, because people have written and said, 'I'd like to know what else you've written; I want to find it,' and I can write back and say, 'So sorry; you can't lay hands on it.' I made myself go back and read the book, thinking, 'Oh my God, if someone should lay hands on it, what will they be reading?' So I went back and read it and thought, 'Okay, I do stand by the writing.' But I really cringed over the subject matter. In a first novel, you are usually revealing your own personal pain in fictional form, and my novel came out of a lot of upheaval in myself. I think it was just very thinly disguised upheaval—that's what it was."

Popham also speaks freely about the pain of going unpublished for sixteen years, after *A Blank Book in 1974,* and of "that dry spell between publications when I was an active writer, a daily writer. I let all of my contacts and friendships lapse with writers like Tom McGuane and Al Young and others, because of a sense of humiliation at going unpublished. I didn't want to be a coattail friend. . . . We all started out on a par" at Stanford in the prestigious Wallace Stegner program, "but I had to contend with the sense of humiliation that one feels professionally at rejection," the feeling that her lack of publication was embarrassing for them and for her. She says that "one of the first things I felt when *Skywater* was accepted, on that first day, was that my chin came up. My chin came up! I had been so down for so long. I had been so cloistered really, arms'-lengthening myself from other writers who sort of feel they need to say, 'How's it going? Anything in the offing?' and always hearing 'No, nice letters of rejection,' and so on. It's just been wonderful to get back in touch with old friends and resume contact."

There was also the story of a novel that Popham finished in 1976. "A major New York publisher was close enough to acquiring it that they asked me to come to New York and talk to them about some changes. At that time *Looking for Mr. Goodbar* by Judith Rossner was riding high and my book also had an attempted rape scene in it. All the editors who had read the book were riveted by this scene, and they wanted me to [enlarge] the violent side of my book. Somebody's nose was saying, 'This literary book can be made really commercial if the author will beef up more of this stuff.' " But Popham declined to do it. "It cost me publication and that book never saw the light of day."

At this moment the interviewer feels the urge to applaud. But Melinda Popham doesn't let herself off that easily. "Would I have done this if someone had said to me: 'This is your only chance to get this book published?' Would I have done it? I don't know. At that point not many people had seen it, and this was a book that my agent was sure was going to be published." Popham is now rewriting it because "again, it's a book that won't let go of me." Although "it's not an environmental book about animals and is about urban relationships, it is really thematically related because there is the same sense of spiritual quest coming through it. I'm obviously sort of obsessed with immortality."

Popham, who believes that "women pay more attention to their dreams and to their memories" than men, says that "there's a funnel in our heads, and if you picture experience just going in the big part of a funnel, only a certain part of experience comes down to become memory. We don't, in fact, remember everything we experience. So what makes it down the neck of the funnel has to be the most powerful of that huge bucket of experience; it's already getting distilled in having to move down. . . . Maybe at the bottom of the funnel there's even a little meshed screen that filters out still more, so that what finally comes through are just these little grains of experience that are the memories that you work with." In any case, Melinda Popham does not see herself "as someone who buries memories. I don't avoid pain by not remembering something; I try to remember. I don't mean that I wallow in it, but I try to remember. Memory is empowering, and it's what gives you your sense of continuity in the world."

Melinda Worth Popham seems to me to be very much like Hallie, the female character in *Skywater*, whom she describes as "not a hermit, but a woman who acts with civility and decency and kindness towards those around her even if they happen not to be human." Like Hallie, all of her "relationships are humane relationships." This was revealed especially in a story she told me about the day *Skywater* was finally accepted for publication.

Her children, who are "boomingly proud" of her, "hadn't been through all sixteen years, but they'd seen me go through the rejection of the first round of *Skywater*, and they were around when the news came [from her agent] that the book probably wasn't going to get published. So, when Graywolf took the book, I went to pick them up. . . . (They go to an Episcopal church school and there is a little prayer garden off to the side of the church.) I parked in the parking lot, took them by the hands, and said, 'Come with me.' They were sort of worried that they were in trouble (they were then eight and ten), but I sat them down on this bench and knelt down in front of them so I could see both of their faces. I said, '*Skywater* is going to be published.' My son just came off the bench—it reminded me of how Mary Martin as Peter Pan was yanked up by guy wires—my son went up into the sky. I just looked up at him and he was up in the sky saying, 'It's wonderful, it's wonderful.' And then I looked over at [my daughter] Lilly, and she had covered her face with her hands and burst into tears. She said, 'Oh, Mom, your sadness has ended.' " Popham realized, as have many writers with children, "how much they know. Although they had never acted as if they [knew] how very depressed I was, I'm so glad they have gotten to see me have my happiness happen. It has been an object lesson for them to see that hard work pays off.

"The thing is," she mused, "writing is the spine of my life. And to have publication denied for so long was to be denied the completion of the process."

BOOKS BY MELINDA WORTH POPHAM

NOVELS

A Blank Book. New York: Bobbs-Merrill, 1974.
Skywater. Saint Paul, Minn.: Graywolf Press, 1990; Ballantine, 1991.

Photo Credits